(19297/69)

bor
of
afte
by

2.

D1428866

Modern Iceland

Also by John C. Griffiths

The Survivors, 1965

Afghanistan, 1967

Modern Iceland

JOHN C. GRIFFITHS

PALL MALL PRESS · LONDON

Published by The Pall Mall Press Ltd.
5 Cromwell Place, London, SW7

FIRST PUBLISHED 1969

© JOHN C. GRIFFITHS, 1969

SBN 269 67182 x

Printed in Great Britain by
The Garden City Press Limited,
Letchworth, Hertfordshire

*For Timothy and Christopher
on their first foreign journey*

Contents

Acknowledgements

In writing this book I have been indebted to the many Icelanders who lavished their time, knowledge and hospitality on me during my travels in all parts of their country. I am most grateful to Halldor Laxness, Professor Sigurdur Thorarinsson, Bjarni Jonsson and his colleague Hallgrimur Snorrason of the Economic Institute. They all not only spent much time in discussion with me but were kind enough to read the draft of the sections of the book relevant to their interests and make many constructive suggestions on it. I owe a particular debt to Thor Vilhjalmsson who not only read the entire manuscript and commented at length upon it but helped greatly in putting me in touch with writers and artists. I am grateful to Dr Jennifer Chandler for her helpful comments on the draft and to Bjarni Gudmundsson for the many contacts, including my interview with the prime minister, which he arranged for me. Finally, I must express my appreciation of the patience of my wife and two older sons who accompanied me on my last visit and complained of my digressions and distractions neither then nor subsequently.

Note on Icelandic Currency and Monetary Figures

During the period of little over a year in which this book was being written Iceland twice devalued its currency, once in November 1967 by 24·6 per cent, again in November 1968 by 35·2 per cent. I have, therefore, adhered to prices expressed in terms of those prevailing in June 1967 and at the pre-November 1967 exchange rate, unless expressly stated otherwise.

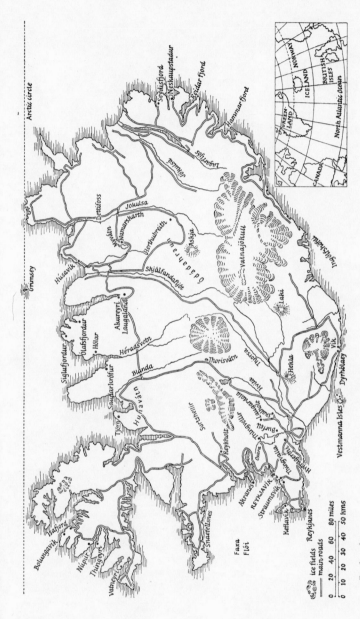

Iceland

Prologue

THERE WAS a woman called Guthny Gilsdottir. In 1959, when she was nearly seventy years old, she left the city of Reykjavík to return to the place of her birth. This was a small farm three miles beyond the village of Núpur in the north-western fjords.

The farmhouse was not large, no more than eight yards square. Nor was it warmly packed with the dozen people who had lived there in her girlhood. For she was now alone, cut off from her neighbours except for a telephone (whose bell, elsewhere imperative, she ignored) and a tractor which in winter, through several feet of snow, she stubbornly drove to mass in Núpur on the appropriate Sundays.

She had returned to her farm to find peace: a peace age could not find in the noise and hurry of Reykjavík, which she regarded as having an undesirably 'American' pace of life. At the farm she finds the peace of nature. There she has her roots, a sense of belonging in a home whose wood and concrete walls were erected in 1894 round the thick-walled structure of turf which had stood there before. Her family had farmed in this place since 1820. The family itself she traces with faultless memory, generation by generation, to 1700. Many Icelanders will unerringly retrace their heredity to the twelfth or eleventh centuries.

As Guthny remembers these things, her face becomes animated, reflects excitement, an undiminished capacity for extracting humour and pleasure from the trivia, even the inconveniences, of daily life in simpler times, a stoic acceptance of its inescapable calamities. She betrays little sign of age, save an occasional tug to bring her woollen cardigan down over her wrists or settle it more comfortably around her neck. Her memory of fifty years ago is exact down to the last detail of the daily and yearly cycle of life.

It was a cycle dictated by the seasons and crowded in every minute. The sea rather than the land fed and kept them, for the few sheep and one or two cows would have offered but a poor livelihood for her father's family, let alone for the other two families which lived on his land and pastured their own animals there. Fishing began in March, with the first faint easing of winter, for the rock salmon in the pools. In April or May, after the lambing, her father would take out his smaller boat, manned by the farmhands of the other two families who laboured on the land and crewed at sea. These boats were kept in boathouses at the tip of the Ness, a good walk beyond the farm; but a good walk was better than a long row. The fish caught now were washed, sorted, then dried in the sun. To fetch the best price, they had to be cured white, not burnt yellow, which meant that the women had to spread them out on the stones, turn them regularly and gather them up into piles, perhaps four or five times a day whenever rain threatened.

The bulk of the fish, after the families' supplies had been laid in, was then sold across the fjord in Thingeyrí. From that great metropolis, numbering some 400 inhabitants, they bought only flour, coffee and sugar. Clothes were homespun and shoes made from catfish skins.

In July and early August, the men came ashore for the hay-making and to gather in the flocks from the mountains for the winter. And then, this time with a larger boat and a few extra hands, hired for the job, making a crew of eight or ten in all, they put a little farther out to sea to lower their nets and trail their lines. This deeper fishing they continued even into the dark and storm-hazardous days of early December. The fish so caught was sold wet, not dried.

Once winter set in with full severity, confining all to their homes, life eased a little; but it was not idle. The men made and mended farm and fishing gear, the women worked the wool of their own sheep through every stage to the finished garment. Upwards of 200 feet of cloth would be worked into cloth in any one year in Guthny's family, where each woman was given 20 feet of material and every man the same length made up into clothes. Right up to Guthny's day, and ever since Saga times, the basic unit of measure and value among the Icelanders was an ell of 'homespun'.

While they worked, they entertained themselves. One member of the family would read aloud. With a shrewd eye to economy, this reader changed every year, being a member of the family old enough to read but too young to work. Reading and writing were learned from the mother, grandfather or grand-mother, or perhaps even one of the farmhands; and occasion-ally the priest would call to see what progress was being made. On weekdays, the readings would be from the Sagas; on Sundays, from books of sermons written specially for this pur-pose. When it grew too dark to weave or read, the women would knit and everyone joined in singing folk songs.

Such a life would not seem to leave much spare time for the

luxury of courtship; but, said Guthny, 'Nature has always had its means'. Sometimes there were free days and horseback expeditions to gather berries on the hillsides, to visit neighbours, and to see and be seen. After the turn of this century, societies (such as the Templars) provided further opportunities for young people to meet and for all to create their own entertainment. This was a life whose key was self-sufficiency.

Guthny is alone on her farm now. Her husband, a retired ship's engineer in Reykjavík, returned to his old ship for one day to help out when his successor fell ill. The ship went down with all hands. Guthny is cheerful but no optimist in her philosophy, and she regrets the passing of the self-sufficient life. Her belief is that material prosperity may work against independence of mind and spiritual values, particularly the spirit of Christianity; as the one increases, the others diminish. The time may then come when, as a direct consequence of the decline in individualism, self-sufficiency and moral fibre, economic decline also sets in and with it, more sinisterly, the decay of those features which have hitherto embodied the Icelandic national character.

The life to whose vestigial traces Guthny still clings was commonplace in Iceland until the Second World War. Thereafter, in less than a decade, Iceland travelled through a millennium's changes. Great pains now have to be taken to preserve the last few examples of the buildings, utensils and personal belongings which, only a quarter of a century ago, were those of every Icelander.

The purpose of this book is to try, as far as possible, to identify that 'Icelandic national character' which Guthny prizes so highly, to appraise the influences which have shaped it in the past and affect it in the present, and to determine whether or not Guthny Gilsdottir will be right in her foreboding.

I

The Beautiful Nightmare

THE ICELANDERS are a people shaped not so much by their natural environment as by their determination to overcome it. Sigurdur Thorarinsson has described it as a thousand-year struggle against fire and ice.[1] While this strikes a dramatic antithesis between the subterranean fires and the great icecaps and snowfields through which they often break, it does not quite define the truly critical element in the formative natural forces at work in Iceland: the element of water, of *vatn*. Certainly, the form in which the power of water is made manifest is sometimes influenced by fire, but it is essentially water itself which, even in its less obviously spectacular forms, conditions the way the Icelanders live, not only materially but spiritually and mentally.

Geologically, Iceland is an infant, a mere 20 million years old: a geologist's living model of so many of the forces which have shaped and still shape the world.

Approximately one-eighth of its surface of 39,808 square miles (which makes it Europe's second largest island) is covered by glacial ice and snow. The glaciers are receding, it is true, but the dominant features of the landscape are still such masses as Vatnajökull, the largest glacier, which covers 3,125 square miles and is well over 3,000 feet thick. (The first person known to have crossed it was an eccentric Englishman, Watts, in 1874.) When a volcanic eruption occurs under its surface, the 'glacier-burst' spews forth overwhelming floods of water, with rocks and blocks of ice which destroy everything in their path and leave behind, among the great boulders strewn over the plain-like wandering riverbeds, the few rounded objects in Iceland's harshly linear and angular landscape.

Almost another one-eighth of the country is covered by lava deposited since the last Ice Age (i.e., within the last 20,000 years). On the longitudinal axis, Iceland lies on the rift in the earth's surface beneath the Atlantic which runs from Jan Mayen Island in the north to the tip of South America, throwing up islands along its line from north to south, and causing such volcanic upheavals as the eruption on Tristan da Cunha in 1961. The east, west and part of the north of Iceland are the creation of alpine folding, part of the line of basaltic lava which stretches from Greenland through Iceland and the Faroes to northern Europe. At the end of the Tertiary period (some 2 million years ago), only the Icelandic volcanoes, at the junction of these two ruptures of the earth's surface, were still regularly active, continuing to build long ridges and table–mountains of breath-taking grandeur in a landscape of impermanence and uncertainty.

The central desert, the Odádahraun—'desert of evil deeds', refuge of outlaws and heroes—is one of the most lifeless places in the world. So alien is its aspect, so totally inimical to the survival of man is its barrenness, that it is used as a training ground for American astronauts to acclimatise them to survival on the moon.

Uniformity might be expected in such a volcanic landscape, but its variety is incredible. Nearly every morphological type of volcano known is to be found in Iceland: cone volcanoes, of which the most famous example is Fujiyama in Japan; shield volcanoes, like those to be found in Hawaii; great fissure eruptions up to eighteen miles in length; box volcanoes, such as Askja (which means 'box' in Icelandic)—all are liberally exemplified.

The area around Myvátn in the north-east has all the fascinating beauty of a nightmare. By the shores of Myvátn ('Midge Lake'), dead midges, which bred on its warm waters, are sometimes piled so thickly that car wheels spin helplessly, unable to grip the road. Lumps of pocked lava stand out in and around the lake like action-sculpture impatiently tossed together in shapes which trap the morbid fancy into ever more shivering excursions. Eastward, away from the lake, the road crosses a lava-field where steam seeps from innumerable cracks like the mist created by rain on a warm tarmac. The tower of the diatomite plant gazes insecurely across the road at a jet of steam spurting thirty feet out of a curved iron pipe which is treated as nonchalantly by the local inhabitants as a village pump used to be in nineteenth-century England: inhabitants who derive pleasure from the apparent hostility of the landscape, bathing naked in the blood-warm sulphate-blue waters of an underground spring while a flurry of late June snow whisks past in a brief blizzard.

The road climbs steeply for a few hundred feet, looking as if it had been cut through the new red ash of a municipal tip; then over the hump and down the other side to the sulphurous odours of Namarskarth. The red now has a browner hue, streaked with green and yellow and encrusted white along the fissures which split the side of the tip like cracks in the skin

7

of an over-ripe plum. Steam leaks from their length or gushes from the ground in endless vertical jets a few feet beyond a drunkenly leaning notice, faded red on peeling white, which warns in English: 'Danger. Keep out.' No one does. Beyond again, where the darker colours are—the orange, brown, dark blue and black spectrum of damnation—the ground undulates and heaves, bubbles of mud stretch and burst as if about to swell up in a glutinous embrace and absorb the errant soul which dares to look unmoved on such torments.

The road spins away again. A left turn to the north follows a track which disappears in shifting desert sands (which ought by rights to lie 5,000 miles away to the south-east) towards Dettifoss, where casual chunks of basalt have been piled up to make a grandstand for Europe's most powerful waterfall. Or you can swing right and south towards Askja, the box volcano set in the bitterly grim waste of Ódádahraun. The track wanders across a desert of fine grit and another of cracked lava slabs towards the glorious breast of Herdubreid. Blue and darker blue, the mountain grows straight up from the surrounding plain, tapering finely to a nipple of white snow sharp against the pale, pale blue of the sky. As you move towards it, Herdubreid seems to stand there with no change in size for hours. Then suddenly it looms up on your right and gives way to reveal the higher, more terrible but less majestic peaks of Askja beyond.

Even a Landrover has to be abandoned in the snow with the summit of Askja still a long way distant. The way upward curls past the long tongue of clinker which marks the flesh of the mountain like an ill-healed scab. Volcanic eruptions in Iceland heal slowly, and Askja's last violent eruption was in 1961. Gently steaming craters still mark the upward line to the top. The ash is new, the clinker scarcely set. It looks all light and crumbling; eventually it will become a compacted black carapace. The colours in its dark composition have not yet settled to their final shade and disposition. It is a hard climb.

The snow crust at any moment may break to thrust you against the sharp rock beneath; boots and limbs are soon lacerated. And at the top, what but more miles of snow, ice, volcanic rock —and a lake within the Askja box, threequarters of it covered by ice, which has before now swallowed the sacrilegious hydrographer who dared to measure its depths. Great banks of yellow cloud come mounting up the horizon like a huge industrial smog. It is time to hurry down the mountainside, clamber back into the Landrover and seek shelter in the nearest tourist hut. It stands perched beside the ice-cold stream running off Herdubreid, a small wooden refuge erected for holiday pleasure by Icelanders for whom these nightmare wonders and their weird beauty are the 'stuff that life is made of'.

The volcanoes of Iceland at their present rate of lava output would build another island of the same size in a million years but for the almost equally fierce forces of erosion—frost, wind and sea—continually tearing at its structure. Vegetation and habitation alike are rarely found above the 600-foot contour, and never above 1,800 feet. One has only to spend a few days in these deserts to see how well justified was the Icelander's estimating an outlawed hero's true courage by the time he was able to survive in such a wilderness.* But there could be no better place to hide, so riddled with crevices and caverns are the cracked acres of lava. The hunters would need almost to stumble over a man before they found him; while he, from a modest vantage point, could see them approaching from miles away across those great open expanses, almost without horizon, which are the characteristic landscape of Iceland and without which the Icelander seems to feel claustrophobically cooped up. Lacking accurate directions, we spent several hours vainly searching for the entrance to one such famous hideaway, Surtshellir, through which, legend has it, a bemused outlaw once

* e.g. Grettir in *Grettirs Saga* who survived twenty years in the wilderness when outlawed; and more recently, Eyvinder of the mountains, inspiration for Icelandic drama and a classic Swedish silent film.

wandered in the darkness to emerge a long time later, many, many miles away, with his shoes filled with gold-dust.

An Icelander seems to live despite the land, not off it, and this same passionate instinct for survival is reflected in the plant life which forays into the fringes of the central desert areas. As your Landrover comes ponderously crashing down over the ten-thousandth fold of lava, which tumbles it in a moment from a skyward-pointing rocket to a burrowing mole, you think the jarring has affected you physically with dancing coloured spots before the eyes. There, growing out of the harsh brown rock, is a bright, impertinent clump of pink flowers. Such flowers—all of a miniature, intricate delicacy which contrasts so poignantly with the gigantesque surroundings—can be found in many varieties all over Iceland.

In a sense, the volcanoes, the lava fields, the great basalt cliffs and ravines, the glacial boulders, are the dead flesh of the country. It is water which is the animating spirit of this great lump of earth-forged clinker that would otherwise be a dead outcasting of rubbish. Water, threading its way down a thousand streams and rivers, boiling through narrow ravines, thudding like blood in the ears over great waterfalls, spouting at boiling point from the earth, lying still and tempting in deep blue warm springs, frozen in slabs of cake icing on the mountains, drizzling continuously out of the grey skies and, always, nuzzling, caressing, smashing, harrowing the coasts with its warm Gulf-stream touch in the south-west and its Arctic stroke in the north-east—water gives life to Iceland. The volcanoes and their continual outpourings of lava have thrust that life back to a green fringe round the edge of the island, back to a green fringe and beyond it to the sea.

Civilisations rose up in the rest of Europe, but these seas long remained unknown to man. Probably the first men to see Iceland were those whose adventures are described in the quasi-biographical *Navigatio Sancti Brendani*, compiled in the early tenth century and purportedly referring to Irish missionary activity in the sixth century. There it is related that the saint and his companions sailed near to a smoking mountain which rose from the sea and whose inhabitants hurled lumps of burning clinker after the fleeing brethren who devoutly believed they were quitting the sulphurous mouth of Hell.

The belief that Iceland, and more particularly the volcano Hekla, housed the mouth of Hell was widespread for many centuries. As late as the seventeenth century, the French traveller Martinière was firmly convinced that he could hear the shrieks of damned souls shivering in the pack-ice where the devil had left them to cool off before returning them to the fires of Hekla.

Travellers continued to be overawed by the wonders of Iceland and its coastal waters. In 1793, a Danish captain was amazed by the sight of a submarine eruption.

At three o'clock in the morning, we saw smoke arising from the sea and thought it to be land; but on closer consideration we concluded that this was a special wonder wrought by God and that a natural sea could burn. . . . When I caught sight of this terrifying smoke, I felt convinced that Doomsday had come.[2]

An anonymous Victorian writing in mid-century was depressed rather than overawed by Iceland's bleak appearance.

Few countries present a more repulsive aspect than this land of snows, which even in its external figure bears the marks of those convulsions that deform its surface. It looks like the fragment of some former world that has alone escaped destruction, confirming the opinion which regards it as a portion torn from the bottom of the sea by the expansive energies of fire. Its dark rugged coasts sometimes rise into lofty precipices, against which the ceaseless waves beat in vain; at other times, the rocks rent asunder give place to long narrow fjords, in whose calm waters the mariner, escaping from the stormy ocean, finds a safe retreat. The southern side alone is flat and sandy. But there also numerous shoals, quick sands, and breakers, expose the poor fishermen to great danger, and render it almost impossible to land in safety. From Hammar Fjord to Ingólfshöfdi long banks of sand, some of them nearly two miles broad, guard the shore, and in other parts numerous rocks or skerries defend it from the waves.[3]

Today, if you sail to Iceland from Britain, the first thing you see is a neatly spaced line of small fishing-boats slithering up and down on the Atlantic swell, each evenly quartering its appointed patch of ocean, bright blobs of white like a flare path on a landing strip. There, at the end of the 'runway', at first no more than a darker patch in the horizon cloudbank, loom out the jutting basalt cliffs of Dyrhólaey, pierced by a great arch: a giant's peephole. The country seems make-believe, for surely so many bizarre, grotesque, extravagant features could not in reality be thrown together in one place. You sail past the Vestmanna Islands, and take for granted the legend that they are the angry missiles hurled there by giant trolls.*

You sail on round the Reykjanes peninsula which occasionally spits from its tip, not some natural rejection of the earth's, but a patrolling aircraft from the American base at Keflavík. Then, crossing the southern stretch of the great bay of Faxa Flói, you put into Reykjavík harbour to anchor in disbelief before a scene from a child's picture-book: a toytown of roofs of every shade of green and red, a pattern of bright spots like those in a colour-blindness test-chart. And round and behind the city stand the hills and mountains, which can be seen on a clear day even as far as Snaefellsnes, seventy miles away across

* There is a most graphic drawing of this by Asgrimur Jonsson, the original of which is in his home at Reykjavik.

Faxa Flói: mountains which have been the subject of heated debate between candidates in a municipal election who disagreed as to their beauty.

It is a thrill not untinged with trepidation to venture on shore in the face of the ceaselessly buffeting wind which is to be your inescapable companion for as long as you stay. If there exist anywhere switching points in a space–time continuum when the traveller moves from one time-belt and scale to another, then Iceland, where past, present and future are often almost indistinguishable, must be one of them. It is almost a relief to be plunged into the stresses and annoyances, common to any modern city, that are the everyday reality of Reykjavík.

⊠

Now, as in the past, Iceland initially arouses disturbing, if superficial, reactions in men from more temperate lands. But one line of voyagers, more accustomed to inhospitable landscapes, persevered and penetrated the daunting outward appearances to discover a land which their descendants would love with a passion unsurpassed anywhere else in the world.

Iceland's full entry into history became inevitable with the spread of Viking power from Scandinavia in the ninth century and of that adventurous Nordic spirit on which no horizon could set limits. The piratical Viking kingdoms spread to the Orkneys and Shetlands, the Faroes, the north of Scotland, the Western Isles, the Isle of Man and Ireland; and the sea coasts of Wales and England received their longships and often their settlements. The Vikings braved the Atlantic wastes to reach North America. Their vessels prowled down the rivers of Russia to the Black Sea and to Mundberg, Constantinople, itself.

Most of the first settlers in Iceland, in the ninth century, were Norwegians. A few came from Denmark, Sweden and the northern Celtic fringes of Britain, but even these were often closely related to the main families from Norway, who headed the settlement, thus establishing the importance of kinship in subsequent Icelandic society. To this ethnic mainstream was added the Celtic blood of the Vikings' slaves and women, often captured in raids on the coasts of Ireland and Britain and brought to Iceland and replenished as necessary. The mixture of Celt and Scandinavian has created a race in which the women are often of startling beauty, with the muscular agility of the Scandinavians, but on a far lighter and more slender scale, tempered and animated with the vivacity of the Celts. Here and there a startling redhead or dark eyes and dark hair give an attractive reminder of this mixed descent. The men seem to fall into two distinct groups: the tall, fair, blue-eyed Scandinavians, and the dark stocky Celts—both far more reserved, even taciturn, than their loquacious womenfolk. Spanish, French and other fishermen have added their dash of flavouring to the national types. These divisions are, of course, purely genetic. In the eleven hundred years of Iceland's settlement, a completely homogeneous Icelandic race and nation have been formed.

The period of the settlement and the three and a half centuries which followed, though dubbed a 'Golden Age' by the Icelanders themselves, might well have been called the Age of Carelessness. Accustomed to the almost inexhaustible forests of their own country, the settlers ravaged the scant woods of Iceland.

The dwarf birch and willow, which are virtually all Iceland can now boast in the way of trees, suffered the same way, for they provided a ready source of fuel. As a result, the modern visitor is now proudly shown a scruff of small trees (which scarcely deserves the name of copse) as if it were a forest. The Icelanders are guiltily conscious of what their forebears have done, and a calculated policy of reafforestation in recent times is at least a gesture of restitution. It is thus the more surprising to observe the profligacy with which the modern Icelander uses timber (every stick of which still has to be imported) for fencing, roadside workmen's fires and even the extensive scaffolding for building houses—although the houses themselves are now primarily constructed of concrete. Depradations by the livestock which the refugees brought were even more serious, for they constituted a major upheaval in the ecological balance of the country in which herbivorous animals had been completely unknown.

It would be unjust to overemphasise the damage done by the early settlers for, as is clear from the Sagas, from the very beginning they had to send home for timber for any large-scale projects such as building ships and houses. Isolation from the wind- and bird-borne seeds of trees that might grow in such a climate and the climate itself are the principal factors accounting for the lack of trees and heavy vegetation. However, the settlers and their animals undoubtedly accelerated the process of erosion which today disfigures so much of Iceland.

Nature was not content to revenge herself by the mere stripping of the soil. The severance of historical, political and commercial ties with the Scandinavian mainland in the thirteenth and fourteenth centuries, and the impoverishment of the agricultural land by overcropping and overfelling, coincided from the thirteenth century with the onset of nearly 400 years of virtually unrelieved natural disaster, starting with earthquakes and a major eruption of Mount Hekla (AD 1300).

Certainly this was not the first time that Hekla had erupted—its first recorded outburst was in 1104—and the phenomenon of volcanic eruption is one with which Icelanders of all ages have been almost contemptuously familiar, since they occur on average every five years. But the eruptions of Hekla, the 'Mouth of Hell', are particularly awesome. The lava flow on the last occasion, in 1947–48, was on the first day greater than the volume of water poured into the sea by most of Europe's largest rivers.[4] The Victorian writer referred to on page 11, quoting earlier authorities, described an eruption of Hekla in 1766 in these terms:

Masses of pumice, six feet in circumference, were thrown to the distance of ten or fifteen miles, together with heavy magnetic stones, one of which, eight pounds in weight, fell fourteen miles off, and sunk into the ground though still hardened with frost. The sand was carried towards the north-west, covering the land a hundred and fifty miles round four inches deep, impeding the fishing boats along the coast and darkening the air so that at Thingore, 140 miles distant, it was impossible to know whether a sheet of paper were white or black. . . . Where the ashes were not too thick it was observed that they increased the fertility of the grass fields, and some of them were carried even to the Orkney Islands, the inhabitants of which were at first terrified by what they considered showers of black snow.[5]

But the mounting catastrophes which began with the Hekla eruption of 1300 were by no means solely geological. Between 1402 and 1404, some two-thirds of the population died in an epidemic of the Black Death, one of several to sweep the island in the fifteenth century. What had been in 1100 a flourishing, wealthy community of 80,000 had become by 1801 a mere 47,212 souls crushed by abysmal poverty and barely managing to keep alive. Not until a full century later did the population regain even its twelfth–century level, the 1901 census figure being 78,000. During this period, moreover, the climate deteriorated sharply, the drift ice from the Arctic gripping more of the coast more often. So cold did it become that all attempts to grow cereal crops were abandoned.

The houses in which the Icelanders lived reflected the change in their fortunes. The long houses of the early settlers, the *mise en scène* for so many of the clashes of the Sagas, were relatively luxurious by contemporary standards. Their timbered halls were hung with tapestries and shields, and heated by great burning fires running the length of the room. But these houses were superseded by grim hovels of stone and turf where there was scarcely room for a man to stand upright, let alone for the status-bestowing 'seat' with its high pillars denoting the importance of the master of the house. Supplies of fuel dwindled and the diet became restricted to the home-procured staples of fish and mutton.

Then, in 1783, there occurred one of the most terrifying eruptions of all time, that of the volcano Laki. For seven months it poured out its lava over 220 square miles—enough, as Professor Thorarinsson so graphically puts it, 'to cover the whole of Switzerland to a depth of a foot'. This was the largest stream of lava ever recorded. The blue haze it created was seen not only all over Europe, but even in Asia. In Iceland itself, its sulphurous precipitations completely poisoned plant life over a huge area, killing off, as a result, much of the island's cattle (an effect it had even as far away as the Orkneys). In the ensuing famine, one-fifth of the already decimated population died.

But from then on the climate gradually improved. Until the late 1960s, the pack-ice had been almost totally absent for many decades. The eruptions which have occurred (with the dramatic exception of Hekla in 1947–48) have been in the deserts far from human habitation, or in the sea, as when the flaming island of Surtsey was born in 1963. For the Icelanders these awesome natural phenomena are not, in fact, a cause of dread, of nervous anticipation of a hundred possible disasters, but rather of curiosity, even of pride and excitement. No sooner does an eruption start than the slopes of the volcano in question swarm not only with geologists and geomorphologists, dodging the bombardment of *ejecta* to gather samples and take temperatures and other readings, but with curious sightseers. An eruption (if not an earthquake) has become something you measure or admire rather than from which you run away. After all, the possibilities for flight in Iceland are somewhat limited; there is nowhere to go from an Ultima Thule.

2

Commonwealth and Colony

THE ULTIMA THULE of classical literature has been attributed to many places at various times.* The earliest references, from Strabo and Tacitus to Claudian, probably placed it in northern Britain and peopled it with Picts. Procopius and Jordanes shift it to Scandinavia; and later, from the ninth century AD, these earlier locations having become too familiar, the monastic writers of Britain and Ireland transferred it westwards to Iceland. Thus, St Brendan's pious hope (as formulated in the *Navigatio Sancti Brendani*) that Ultima Thule would be-

* Scholars differ widely on this matter, but the line of argument put forward by the anonymous author of *An Historical and Descriptive Account*, referred to in the previous chapter, seems to me the most probable and is followed here.

come known was impossible of realisation; his own probable explorations only served to move it north and west again.* Ultima Thule never had geographical, only psychological, *loci*. It was always the place beyond the farthest known point, the edge of the world. In as much as Iceland seems to occupy a similar place in the European consciousness—emerging stark and clear from the millennial fog banks for a brief moment as protagonist in a 'cod war' or scene of a shipwreck—it can lay better claim than most to the title 'Ultima Thule'.

No precise date can be ascribed to the discovery of Iceland, although the beginnings of permanent human settlement are clearly chronicled. The evidence of a few Roman coins, of the latter part of the third century AD, suggests that perhaps the ships of Carausius, governor of Britain under Diocletian, ventured out so far into the northern waters. And, to judge from the *Navigatio Sancti Brendani*, there is a strong possibility that Irish sailors were familiar with these waters. Allowing for the delightful embellishments of which, even in those days, the Irish were masters, and the fact that at that time Iceland was probably not inhabited, the description in the *Navigatio*, quoted on page 11 above, could well have been of a volcanic eruption near the seashore.

The existence of Irish place-names in fairly large numbers indicates a possibility that the Irish had set foot in Iceland on several occasions from the sixth to the ninth centuries;[1] but there is no trace of any permanent dwellings or settlements. It is argued that, in all probability, any Irish inhabitants of the island were hermits seeking temporary spiritual refuge in its physical isolation; or, alternatively, that the Irish place-names are of later origin and derive from the Irish slaves of the early Norse settlers rather than from the first venturers to the 'infernal regions'.

It is easy to misapprehend the location of Iceland for—while

* Cf. Geoffrey Ashe, *Land to the West* (Collins, London 1962), where a rather different theory is developed.

it can certainly be described as a mid-Atlantic island, only 170 miles from Greenland, a brief stepping-stone on those almost incredible voyages of discovery which first reached out to the New World—it is also a mere 500 miles from the northern coast of Scotland. From Reykjavík to Glasgow is only a couple of hours' journey by air.

❆

In fact, the Vikings first discovered Iceland by accident. In 861, Naddod, a notorious pirate who had secured a retreat for himself from his many enemies in the Faroes, was blown off course when returning home to Norway. He landed eventually at Reydhar fjord; but, finding the island uninhabited, soon set sail again, prompted by a farewell snow-shower capping the mountains to describe the country as Snaeland, 'Snowland'. Three years later, another seafarer, Gardar, a Swede, was also blown off course to the east coast of Iceland and began to make his way cautiously northward round the island to Husavík, thus named because he built a house there in which to winter. The following spring he completed his circumnavigation of what was now called Gardarsholm.

Gardar's favourable report persuaded the Norwegian Flokki to explore its coasts deliberately. Uncertain of his course in those pre-compass days (so the story is related in the *Land-namabók*, the book of the settlement, Ari Frode's detailed and apparently almost contemporary account of the early colonisers and their division of the land), Flokki resorted to Noah's navigational technique, but employed crows instead of doves. Yet although Flokki spent two years exploring the island—having, unlike his predecessors, travelled south-west from a landfall on the east coast—he did not settle at the time, deterred by the loss of his livestock and perhaps also by those floes of pack-ice he discovered in the north and from which he gave the island its present name of Iceland.

Ingólfur Arnarson, the first permanent settler in Iceland,

came of necessity. Ingólfur had provoked increasingly powerful enemies in Norway since he had allowed his closest friend, Leif of the Sword, to marry his sister Helga in preference to other suitors. Each time they defeated one of the jealous and affronted enemies, still more were incensed to revenge. After a preliminary exploration of Iceland from which they returned to gather their followers and belongings, Ingólfur and Leif set sail for good in 874.

They made their first landfall on the eastern reach of the long southern coastline, at what is now known as Ingólfshöfdi. It had not been Ingólfur's intention to land at this point on the coast. Being a religious man, he had brought with him on the voyage the seat-pillars of his house in Norway;* obedient to custom, on nearing land he had tossed them into the sea: where they first touched would be the heaven-approved landing place and the site of his new home. But, before he could follow them to the propitious landfall, a storm broke and he was compelled to beach his boats hurriedly. He thus first set up house at Ingólfshöfdi where the deltaic deposits of the ever-shifting glacial rivers from the Vatnajökull icefields have piled up great long gravel beaches and ridges which offer no shelter to ships. Inhospitable though the shore was, the land beyond was fertile. As soon as winter was over, he sent his servants in all directions to seek for the missing seat-pillars. In their travels, they passed through and left behind all of Iceland's most fertile districts in the south-west, from whose pleasant meadows all the milk and meat from modern Reykjavík are drawn. It was not until three years later that they discovered the pillars after crossing the bleak peninsula of Reykjanes. Resisting the temptation to settle in the softer lands, Ingólfur sailed round the coast to the settlement prescribed for him by the winds and currents.

* The seat-pillars were tall timber columns on which the favourite god was carved, standing on either side of the chief seat in the main hall and projecting some way beyond the roof. The taller the pillars, the greater the social stature of their owner.

If tempted to ignore their augury, his loyalty to the decision of the gods may have been confirmed by the fate of Leif, who had scoffed at the seat-pillars convention and been murdered in the first spring of settlement by the Irish slaves he had tried to use in place of the oxen lacking for his plough. Arriving in the bay, Ingólfur saw inland the rising steam of some of those hot springs which now provide central heating for an entire capital city; and he named the place Reykjavík, 'Smoky Bay'. Thus began the first of Iceland's permanent settlements.

Ingólfur and his small band were not long alone. The Norway of their time was divided into a variety of small kingdoms, each with its own ruling king or jarl. These had been centred in loose federations based on certain *things* (councils), the best-known and most important of which were the Gula *thing* and the Oere *thing*. Harald Haarfarger ('Fairhair'), ambitious both to extend his own material prosperity and to provide for his eight sons, determined to bring these scattered kingdoms under his sole rule, and in so far as he succeeded—not all of them submitted to Harald—might be called the first king of Norway. While the leaders of the Gula *thing* were preoccupied in Scotland and Ireland with extending their influence there, Harald seized their domains in Norway and finally crushed their resistance by victory at the battle of Hafurs Fjord in 872. Since Harald was an adept in the violent methods of conquest of his time, those who had opposed him in the name of their liberty naturally looked on his subsequent measures of government as acts of tyranny. Having already been defeated, they found themselves with no alternative to submission but voluntary exile in distant Iceland. Those who sailed there to settle were not, as with so many immigrants, such as those described on the Statue of Liberty, the 'deprived members' of society but among its best. Nor were they mere predators like the pirate Vikings who had first roamed the northern Atlantic. They were men to whom freedom was paramount, men of great individu-

ality and of sufficient wealth to build and equip the larger ships*
necessary to take livestock and household goods to their new
home.

The period of colonisation ended in 930; and in the Commonwealth which followed, Iceland enjoyed a social system
which was vigorous, even violent, but neither rough nor crude.
The vigour expressed itself in many ways. Iceland's young
men roamed the world in search of adventure as fighters,
poets and scholars. In 982, they discovered Greenland, which
they went on to colonise; and in 1000 sailed on from Greenland
to discover America, although here they failed to settle success-
fully. The Icelanders had a great passion for sporting contests
conducted sometimes with no little animosity by the protago-
nists. But the most frequent occasion for violence was when a
man felt that his honour had been slighted. The most swift
and satisfying form of redress, as far as the Icelander was
concerned, was to kill your calumniator. The relatives of the
slain man were almost certain to respond in like manner, and
the blood feud thus became a dominant feature of life in the
Commonwealth of Iceland, although diminished a little in the
first century and a half after the conversion to Christianity.
Such a feud was ended only when an agreed sum of blood money
was accepted by the most recently aggrieved party.

Their religion, like their code of conduct, was simple. The
settlers brought with them the Asa faith, worshipping the gods
of Asgard, among whom the Icelanders' particular favourite
seemed to be Thor. But these deities were far from almighty,
being endowed by their worshippers with the same failings and
frustrations to which they themselves were prone. The gods
were less immediate, however, than the spirits thought to
possess the streams and waterfalls, rocks and trees of the
countryside. Almost animist in their outlook towards their

---

* 'Larger' is a relative term only, for their biggest ship was probably not
above ten tons.

environment, the Icelanders were continually trying to propitiate these local spirits.

But these simple aspects of Icelandic life should not be allowed to convey a misleading impression of a primitive society, for this was far from the case. As is clear from the Sagas, a high standard of cultural, material and intellectual wealth was enjoyed. The settlers, few in number, were drawn almost exclusively from the leading chiefly families of their countries of origin—apart from such slaves as they took with them. They therefore possessed as a whole an uncommonly high level of culture and literacy. The strong oral tradition—by which Icelandic poets were to flatter their way into the esteem of many vain kings in the next few centuries—was backed by the ability of most citizens to read and write, many in Latin as well as in their own tongue. A fine quality of craftsmanship in wood, metal and cloth was also preserved and served to decorate the large and comfortable timber houses of the chiefs and farmers. A vivid picture of this way of life emerges not only from the Sagas, themselves evidence of a long tradition of cultural activity, but in historical and social records, such as the *Landnamabók* and the *Islendingabók*. It is ironic that a civilisation so well chronicled should be so little known in the outside world.

❀

As we have seen, Iceland was colonised as a consequence of events in Norway, and its relations with that kingdom were the main external influence on its affairs for the next four centuries. After the early settlement, the Norwegian kings made several attempts to subvert the Icelandic Commonwealth by bribing or coercing important chiefs into trying to persuade their fellow countrymen to acknowledge the Norwegian crown. (It was the Norwegian kings also who initiated the eventually more successful missionary attempts to convert Iceland to Christianity in the tenth century.) The principal mover in this policy was King Olaf Trygvason. Norwegian temporal ambitions were eventually fulfilled in the middle of the thirteenth century when the Icelandic people, sickened and exhausted by the feudal strife which had centred on the Sturlung family for forty years, called on Haakon, then king of Norway, to intervene and restore peace in exchange for their fealty. Snorri Sturlusson—the great Icelandic statesman-historian who was instrumental in thwarting the Norwegian monarch for a while by deceit—paid the price by being murdered beside his hot-spring bath at Reykholt.

The treaty of 1262, in which this agreement was recorded, safeguarded the rights and domestic independence of the Icelanders and the continuation of their laws and customs. It also gave a guarantee of minimal trade with the outside world through Norway. By the end of the thirteenth century in Norway itself, the disputes between the kings of Norway and the archbishops of Trondheim* bordered on open conflict and Iceland became involved as one of a number of marginal issues. The Norwegian kings deprived the Icelandic bishops of their authority and the Church of much of its lands to an extent which prompted the pope to intervene (on behalf of Trondheim rather than Iceland) and express his displeasure in a letter to Eric the Priest Hater, Haakon's grandson, who was then king of Norway. The position of the Church was temporarily eased by the pleadings of the bishop of Skalholt, one of the two sees into which Iceland was then divided, who enjoyed the friendship of the king. But soon papal exactions to finance the Crusades were biting just as deep as the private imposts of the king, and Roman practices, such as celibacy of the clergy and the adoration of images, became the general rule.

The tightening of external authority was furthered by developments in Scandinavia itself. The skilful diplomacy of Queen Margaret of Denmark had, by the union of Calmar in 1397, united the crowns of Norway, Sweden and Denmark first under

---

* The bishoprics of Iceland came first under the see of Bremen and then of Lund before being incorporated into Trondheim.

the 'front man', Eric of Pomerania, then under Margaret herself. Soon a ruling system embracing a foreign governor, sheriffs of the county districts appointed by the Danish king and measures in restriction of trade, placed all genuine authority firmly in the hands of the Danish monarchs. By the seventeenth century, Denmark, its elective system of monarchy replaced by a despotic one and its resources already embroiled in the continual conflict with Sweden which was to last until the end of the eighteenth century, had little time for Iceland. The colony became increasingly impoverished and neglected until, in 1850, Frederick VII restored a free constitution in Denmark and the new régime spread its influence to the Danish colonies.

But if imperial Denmark lost interest in Iceland, a new moulding force was brought to bear on the country from the middle of the sixteenth century onwards: the Reformation. Not that the clergy in Iceland had exhibited that remoteness from their flock which was characteristic of the period in much of the rest of Europe. Indeed, because of Iceland's perennial manpower shortage, they had inevitably been 'of the people', themselves pursuing ordinary rural occupations. In that context they were in sympathy with their parishioners. But the clergy were sometimes imbued with superstition to the point where their parishioners did not know whether to take them for priests or wizards. They also incurred animosity as the instruments of papal taxation on a poor people who, at the start of the sixteenth century, could behold in Iceland a Roman Catholic church at the zenith of its wealth and power.

Even so, had the doctrines of the Reformation depended on popular impetus for their germination they would have grown but little. The Reformation in Iceland was introduced by the clergy themselves. Clerics frequently went to Germany and Denmark for their theological training and study. Here they came in contact with the spirit of the Reformation at its most austere and intense, and many on their return to Iceland began to spread its doctrines in secret. One, Oddur Gottschalksson, even translated the Gospel of St Matthew into Icelandic under the very roof of one of the most vigorous opponents of the Reformation.

Christian III of Denmark, an ardent Lutheran, in 1540 sent one of Oddur's friends, Gissur, to take up the vacant see of Skalholt and spread the new faith in his colony. Gissur gave the clergy liberty to marry again (a restored privilege doubtless much appreciated by the highly sexed Icelanders), setting the example himself. Mass and other Roman practices were shortly after abolished in the see of Skalholt, though still doggedly supported in the see of Holar by Bishop Jon Arason. Arason is one of the most popular figures in Icelandic history, the epitome of patriotism, and his opposition ended only under the executioner's axe. In true Icelandic fashion, his friends avenged his death in blood, but physical resistance to the new teachings soon ceased. The Icelanders in general, however, soon came to take no less exception to the reformed practices than they had to the exactions of the Roman Catholic church, as if sensing instinctively the impending heavy hand of Protestant puritanism which was to crush much of the joy out of their lives. With the abolition of the remaining nine monasteries in 1558, the Lutheran confession was firmly established as the other arm of the yoke of Danish rule. The Church in Iceland thereafter played the same subordinate role to the crown as it did in Denmark itself, and constituted in fact no more than two rather unfavoured bishoprics in the patronage of the king.

For the best part of the next four centuries, the carefree days of the Commonwealth and rule by the Althing were gone.

ꝏ

Although Iceland boasts of being among the first nations to adopt a representative form of government under which an entire nation, without compulsion, agreed in principle to conform to a predetermined code of laws and conduct, the system

27

never sat lightly on the shoulders of the Icelanders. Even in the earliest and most vigorous days of the Icelandic Commonwealth after the first settlement, the rugged individualism of the colonists resulted in a system of government which was frequently a safety-valve rather than a control mechanism.

The first settlers brought with them from Scandinavia the custom of holding *things*, or councils, at which disputes between individual members of the clan or with members of a neighbouring clan were resolved and actions for the common weal discussed and undertaken. When these settlers first arrived in Iceland, there was no shortage of land of which each new arrival could take possession. There was thus little need to convene *things* other than to discuss the problems of a particular limited neighbourhood. These *things* were convened by word of mouth. A wooden mallet, Thor's hammer, later replaced by a cross, was passed by one farmer to his neighbour together with information about the date, place and purpose of the *thing*. The crucial figure at the *thing* was the *gothi*, who was usually the chief of the clan and fulfilled the dual role of judge and priest, presiding at these secular assemblies but also officiating in the temples. The *thing* was usually summoned by the *gothi* himself.

As the settlers grew more numerous, so the activities of each clan impinged more sharply on those of its neighbours. It thus became necessary to create an over-all body to reconcile disputes involving men of several clans, and to establish common laws and common policies in a national interest. The four regional *things* and eventually the Althing above them, were thus created. Iceland claims to have in the Althing the oldest representative parliament in the world; it has met continuously (save for a break in the nineteenth century from 1801 to 1845) since it was founded in 930.

The meetings of the Althing in Commonwealth times showed both a remarkable respect for public opinion and disrespect for the machinery and process of government. Such a paradox is typical of the Icelanders. The present system of government, although far more sophisticated than the ancient Althing, cannot be called ponderous or overbureaucratic. In fact, practically all the ministers of state and their civil servants are housed in a single building in the centre of Reykjavík, originally built in 1764 as a prison for sixteen incorrigible criminals and forty-five more venial offenders. The Icelanders are a truly democratic people in that now, as in their 'Golden Age', the expressed opinions of the entire adult population are a potent factor in determining national policies and, indeed, in sometimes making the business of government unusually difficult.

In 930, the Icelanders decided at the Althing to send the wisest among them back to their land of origin to study its laws and draw up an Icelandic code inspired by them. It is significant that, despite their having fled from what they regarded as the tyrannies of an individual, the Icelanders still sufficiently revered their fatherland's collective traditional wisdom to wish to base their own laws upon it. They accordingly sent Ulfliot, a man of great wisdom, then in his sixties, for a three-year stay in Norway. When he had studied its laws and governmental system, he produced and publicly declared at the Althing the code of laws to govern the Icelandic Commonwealth, thus creating the position of 'lawspeaker'. Subsequently, the lawspeaker was chosen, to serve for a period of three years, at the Althing by the *lögretta*, a meeting at which each *gothi* and two of his followers voted.

The basic unit of law and administration was the *hreppar*, or parish, as it sprung up round one of the original settler chiefs. The old laws stipulated that these should each contain twenty farmhouses or householders. Above the *hreppar* came the counties, then the *things* for each quarter of the country, and at the summit of the structure the Althing. The government of the lowest units was in the hands of men who were in a sense popularly elected local magistrates, being chosen on the basis of wisdom and for their substance. Occasionally, in the case of men of outstanding ability, even a property qualification was waived. As always among the Icelanders, the factor of personal influence was predominant; even at county level and above, where the *gothi* was invariably the local chief, he might not always be the most important man in the district. Status in Iceland depended as much on courage, eloquence, wit and integrity as on material advantages. In any case, the free citizen was quite at liberty to transfer his allegiance to another *gothi*, thus exercising some check on the authority of the chief whose power and prestige were measured by the number of his followers.

The post of *gothi*, once filled by this open-ended system, became largely a hereditary one, passing from father to son until, during the first two centuries of the Commonwealth at least, the shortcomings of such a hereditary *gothi* persuaded the local people to replace him by one more congenial. It was thus usually possible for the post of *gothi* (the *gothard*) to be filled almost democratically; but it could also be disposed of in a commercial transaction by outright sale, or temporarily entrusted to the care of a friend during the *gothi*'s absence. While the power to transfer the *gothard* from one man or family to another was undoubtedly valuable in the heyday of the Commonwealth in maintaining the standards of ability in the office, its abuse in later times was to cause severe trouble for the Icelanders.

The Althing itself met once a year by the shores of Lake Thingvalla at a place now called Thingvellir. The majority of the free population came together for these annual meetings, for it was considered something of a disgrace not to take advantage of one's right to attend. For the local chiefs in particular prestige depended to a large extent on the number of followers they were able to bring with them, the degree of luxury with which they were armed and dressed, and the hospitality made available during the time of the Althing. The women and children came too, for the women enjoyed (and still do) a remarkably high status in Iceland. There was much feasting and sporting contest during the Althing, but its main business was the resolution of disputes, the formulation of any necessary new laws, and—perhaps most important of all, prior to the written codification of the law in the thirteenth century—the recitation by the lawspeaker, chosen by the consensus of his peers, of one-third of the law each year. The lawspeaker also acted as chief judge and presided over the deliberations of the Althing.

If the Sagas are anything to go by, the Icelanders were a litigious lot. Great attention was paid to the forms of the law. It was vital for a man bringing an action against another to have the help of a skilled, albeit amateur, advocate, who would frame the indictment in exactly the right form. If a plea were couched in the wrong terms, the whole case might be vitiated, however just the pleader's cause. The accounts in the Sagas reveal that there was a great deal of verbal fencing, including the extensive use of ridicule, generally by the defendant, to trap an opponent or his advocate into taking a false step. Another critical element in the cases put before the Althing was the use of witnesses. These could, in effect, be subpoenaed, and refusal to give witness carried the penalty of denial of legal rights. Near relations, however, were not permitted to act as witnesses, and all those participating in the proceedings were under oath to act honourably and speak truthfully. These provisions were made additionally important by the fact that, as in many Germanic countries, the witness was not only considered as an objective source of information but, to a great extent, as a character witness; indeed, he almost served the function of juryman as well.

It is not surprising that the decisions of the Althing, reached through such a maze of procedural nicety, were sometimes ignored by litigants who chose to enforce their point of view by the arms of their thingmen (supporters at the *thing*) or in single combat against their adversary. Indeed, at Thingvellir, just as there was a special pool for drowning women in sacks who had been found guilty of such offence as adultery, and a cliff from which witches could be thrown and an island for the beheading of criminals, so there was an island for single combat which limited the possibilities of flight.*

It has sometimes been argued that Iceland was an echo of Athens, a nation whose entire free population† met to discuss matters of national importance, and where every individual citizen had the right to voice his opinions. The analogy, however, is a false one for, despite the similarities in size of population, literary achievement and democratic procedures, the Athenians gave display in public to an incessant pattern of intrigue in an urban society, while the Icelanders met from their widely scattered and isolated communities but once a year. It was this enforced isolation, largely due to the fact that no part of Iceland was sufficiently fertile to sustain for long any large congregation of people, that accounted for the strong sense of personal and individual freedom during the early centuries of the Icelandic Commonwealth. Where the Athenians were by choice interdependent, the Icelanders were of necessity self-sufficient.

⊠

Perhaps the most significant meeting of the Althing in Commonwealth times was that at which the Icelanders, on a single day in the year 1000, adopted Christianity *en masse*. There had been

* *An Historical and Descriptive Account*, previously referred to, records a rather more bizarre mode of single combat, with even less opportunity for flight, in which the two combatants were sealed in a closed vessel with a stick, each with the object of trying to batter the other to death in the dark. But none of my contemporary Icelandic sources could, alas, confirm this.

† There were slaves in Iceland, certainly, until slavery was effectively abolished by the end of the eleventh century; but these were treated rather better than their Athenian counterparts.

individual Christians among the earliest settlers, but they had met with a certain degree of hostility among a people who had brought with them from Scandinavia their own religion and worshipped the gods of Asgard. With the spread of Christianity throughout Norway at the beginning of the tenth century, a number of unsuccessful attempts were made to convert the Icelanders. But, since their system of secular government was very closely interwoven with the administration of the old religion, whose temples were to be found in every major settlement in Iceland, the various piecemeal attempts at conversion to Christianity proved unsuccessful. Towards the end of the tenth century, when Olaf Trygvason was king of Norway, a number of more forceful approaches were made by native Icelanders, backed by Norwegian royal authority, to convert their fellow-countrymen by rather more drastic means. Such missionaries as Stefner, Thangbrand and Thorvald tended to meet resistance to their proselytising with force: never a noticeably successful weapon against the Icelanders.

The willingness of the Icelandic people to discuss in open public debate the respective merits and deficiencies of the two religions (the Asa faith was already being influenced by Christianity) at the Althing and vote for the total adoption of one or the other must be one of history's outstanding examples of rational national behaviour. Despite the excesses of individuals, collectively the Icelanders have always displayed a large and generous tolerance in matters of religion and politics. On the whole, the history of Christianity in Iceland is not marred by the bigotry and persecution which has characterised it throughout the rest of Europe at various times.

To return to the critical meeting of the Althing in 1000: those of the majority and heathen party attempted at first to bar the place of meeting to the Christians, headed by Olaf's emissaries Gissur and Hialti, who had landed a few days before the Althing was to be held in order to state their case. But, gathering their followers, the Christians pressed on and their determination deterred their opponents from attacking them. During the course of the ensuing debate, the Christian party, by a payment of 60 ounces of silver, was able to persuade Thorgir, one of the best-known advocates and himself considered a prominent supporter of the Asa faith, to espouse its case. The story has it that, during the early part of the debate, a messenger ran in to report that an eruption was taking place nearby. The adherents of the old faith immediately declared this to be a sign of the gods' displeasure at the Christian interlopers. Surprisingly Snorri,* another prominent heathen, apparently moved by the Christian case, riposted by asking them with whom the gods had been angry when the awe-inspiring volcanic setting of the Althing itself had been spewed from the earth. This unanswerable argument swayed the audience; after further debate and persuasion by Thorgir, the Althing decided to adopt Christianity as the national religion.

Public worship of the old gods was prohibited but allowed in private. The old temples were pulled down, but eating horse-flesh and the exposing of newborn children was, in theory, still to be permitted. As immediate evidence of their abrupt conversion, the Icelanders proceeded *en masse* to baptism by total immersion, as was the custom then, at the hands of Thormod, the priest who accompanied Gissur and Hialti. But, with a typical touch of realism, a large minority refused to be doused in the icy waters of the Oxara, and insisted on travelling to the warm springs at Laugardala some forty miles away. This combination of esoteric and symbolic argument with realism is typical of the Icelandic character. By 1056, the Icelandic see of Skalholt had been founded, to be followed by the division of the island, ecclesiastically, into two and the foundation of a second see at Holar in 1106.

With the abandoning of the old religion, the Icelanders gave up a number of barbarous customs; although some were initially permitted, they soon fell into desuetude and were subsequently

* Not to be confused with Snorri Sturlusson.

34

banned. In particular, the practice of animal, and occasionally human, sacrifice was abandoned. But it would be a mistake to regard the advent of Christianity as an unmixed blessing. Together with the growing pressures of a rising population on the limited land available, it was responsible for the rapid growth of feudalism and the near-anarchy which followed. Initially, it is true, the influence of the Church was purely beneficial, and there followed within one or two decades of the adoption of Christianity almost a century of peace and the prosperous pursuit of agriculture and fishery. But in 1096, the passing by the Althing of a tithe law (granting to the Church one per cent of a family's substance each year) initiated the process by which the republic was to be destroyed.

The old chief-priest pattern of heathen times was largely perpetuated in the pattern of Christianity in Iceland. The larger churches were built on the land of the great chiefs and remained under their influence. The incumbent was frequently a son of the chiefly family. Since it was customary for priests to marry up to the time Iceland lost its independence, a 'living' could become something of a family inheritance. Indeed, the first bishopric of Iceland, established in 1056, passed from father to son by hereditary right almost as if it were a *gothard*: a practice not, of course, confined to Iceland. Gradually, through the tithe laws, the Church, and hence indirectly the *gothard*, began to accumulate substantial wealth. This was deployed under the old custom to buy out *gothi* after *gothi* until, after a series of mergers and take-over bids, the entire secular and much of the ecclesiastical power was concentrated in the hands of half-a-dozen families, chief among which was the Sturlunga clan. Supported by large hosts of armed retainers, the Sturlungas were able to ignore the rule of law and the Althing, and to disregard the rights and personal liberty of the individual which had formed so vital a part of the structure of the early state.

These conflicts among the great chiefs were further exacerbated in the second quarter of the thirteenth century by the more frequent appointment of foreigners to the bishoprics of Iceland by the archbishop of Trondheim in whose see the island fell. The bishops, anxious to secure their wealth and independence, appealed to their Norwegian metropolitan for support, while the chiefs in their struggles with each other manoeuvred for the favour of the Norwegian king or of prominent jarls. It had long been the ambition of the Norwegian kings to subdue Iceland—refuge of so many domestic troublemakers—to their crown, and they had been none too scrupulous in the means they employed. Their intrigues, however, had been of little avail so long as a reasonable degree of unity and a strong suspicion of foreign influence existed among the Icelanders themselves. From 1230 onwards, the ambition of the contending chiefs overcame their caution and during the next thirty-two years—known as the 'Sturlunga period' after the principal family involved and graphically described in the Saga of that name—they destroyed the independence of Iceland. King Haakon Haakonarson took shrewd advantage of these dissensions, even on one occasion preventing a Norwegian jarl's expedition against Iceland to avoid the risk of its uniting the island's people.

As Haakon had anticipated, leading Icelanders solicited his intervention to restore stability and order. By a treaty of 1262, known as the 'old pact', which followed the defeat of the main Sturlunga factions, Iceland forfeited its independence and acknowledged Norwegian suzerainty. Had Norway retained its own independence perhaps the extensive rights reserved to the Icelanders in the 'old pact' might have been observed. When the kingdoms of Denmark and Norway were united in 1380, Norway's colonies fell under the joint—in effect, Danish—crown: a matter on which the Icelanders were not consulted. The transfer of dominion involved in the rise of the Danish empire, followed by the impact of Lutheranism, soon plunged

Iceland into what most of its people now regard as their 'dark age'.

At the beginning of the sixteenth century, the Roman Catholic bishops were the most powerful people in Iceland. The first of the Reformation bishops, Gissur Einarsson, and the last of those in communion with Rome, Jon Arason, shared in their common passionate love of their country a bond stronger than the divisive force of their doctrinal differences. As elsewhere, the Reformation not only led to such changes as marriage of the clergy* and the translation of the Scriptures into the vernacular, but served also as a pretext for the monarchy to seize Church, and in particular monastic, lands. The Danish kings certainly coveted, and at first claimed, the nine remaining monasteries of Iceland (Benedictine and Augustinian). But, largely through the tact and diplomacy of Gissur, the revenues did not revert to the Danish crown and, for a few years, were used to develop the schools of Iceland. Thus the incipient conflict between Jon Arason and Gissur Einarsson was held in check by their mutual recognition that differences in doctrine were secondary to their common devotion to the good of the Icelandic peoples. But when Gissur died in 1547, Jon soon took to arms to resist his successor to the see of Skalholt and the spread of Lutheran teachings. Violence generated violence, and Jon and his two sons were hastily seized and executed at Skalholt in 1550 by officers of the Danish crown, which dared neither try them on indictment nor deport them to Denmark.

Jon Arason, besides being a considerable poet, brought the first printing press to Iceland in 1526, partly for literary and partly for polemic reasons. It is one of the sharpest ironies of the Reformation in Iceland that on his death the press should

* Jon Arason himself openly maintained a concubine and had many children who had all the privileges of legitimacy and became powerful men in Iceland. This kind of liberal irregularity distinguishes the pre-Reformation church in Iceland.

have been bought by his Lutheran opponents and become instrumental in the dissemination of the new teachings through a series of tracts.

Such were the literary traditions of Iceland and the general availability of a wide range of secular and religious texts in copy manuscript form that the advent of the printed word had nothing like the impact that it achieved in the rest of Europe. During the two centuries before the Reformation, the creation of original literature virtually ceased; and even the writing of annals, a distinctively Icelandic form of literature, was to lapse by the middle of the seventeenth century. But the old literature was carefully preserved and lovingly read, and a considerable quanity of imitative literature, following after the European romances and religious writings, was written. Opinions differ among contemporary critics, some dismissing it as of little worth while others, Laxness among them, believe that the return of the manuscripts which have been kept in Denmark will reveal much of value. Certainly, the return of the manuscripts from Copenhagen, where they have been well preserved for centuries, however unjustly taken in the first place, is arousing great expectations among scholars in Iceland.

With the death of Jon Arason, Iceland lost its last leader against the growing tyranny and exploitation of the Danish kings who, after the Reformation had been fully accomplished, owned, as a result of the expropriation of church lands, approximately one-sixth of the island. The tightening of Denmark's trade monopoly in the seventeenth and eighteenth centuries plunged the country into a steadily greater poverty about which the Danes concerned themselves but little. In 1801, the meetings of the Althing were abolished and its judicial functions taken over by a court of justice in Reykjavík.

The eighteenth century and the first half of the nineteenth are almost entirely devoid of any events of general historical significance in Iceland. The depression and gloom are only occasionally relieved by the bizarre or the farcical. The most colourful of these incidents is undoubtedly that in which an English merchant named Phelps, aided and abetted by a Dane called Jorgen Jorgensen, seized and imprisoned the Danish governor in 1809 and declared Iceland independent under the protection of the British crown. Britain, not it seems in a privateering mood on this occasion, declined this unsolicited acquisition to its dominions and even went so far as to assist the Danish authorities to crush the revolt—if so grand a name for an act of piracy can be justified. It is interesting to speculate what the consequences would have been of uniting Iceland and Britain under the same crown.

Iceland's political fortunes were at their nadir during this century and a half; but, from the middle of the nineteenth century, Icelanders began to reassert themselves. Although the struggle for independence during the nineteenth century was protracted and concrete progress painfully limited, under the leadership of such men as Jon Sigurthsson (died 1879) the national consciousness gathered a momentum which was eventually to prove irresistible. Where there had before been spasmodic individual protests, there was now a growing continuity of organised pressure and dissent. A revival of interest in Iceland's literary heritage, and particularly in its ancient linguistic purity, was an early and major contributory factor in the reawakening of the spirit of national pride and independence. This was reflected in the formation of various literary and cultural societies between 1779 and 1818, the year of the foundation of the National Library, and consolidated a century later with the creation of the University of Iceland in 1911. The purging of the language of Danish derivatives and borrowed terms during this period was symptomatic of the rejection of Danish influences as a whole.

The Althing was re-established in 1843–45, although initially only as a purely consultative assembly, when the Danish colonial power finally acceded to the Icelanders' newly awakened demands for a greater say in their own government. In 1871,

in keeping with the enlightened change in the conduct of their
own affairs, the Danes promulgated a new constitution for
Iceland. This still did not satisfy the new and rapidly growing
demand for full independence, but it did in 1874 lead to the
restoration of the Althing as a legislative power acting jointly
with the crown, although executive authority was still vested
in a governor responsible to a Danish minister and parliament.
With a change of government in 1901 in Denmark, this
grievance was redressed two years later; but it took until 1918
for an Act of Union between Denmark and Iceland to be
agreed and embodied in a new constitution in 1920.

The Act of Union of 1918 and new constitution of 1920 were
the penultimate step in the recapture of independence for
Iceland, for they contained a provision for a revision of the
Act of Union at the end of 1940. This stipulated that, if the
parties did not agree on a new treaty of union within three
years, then the old treaty might be abrogated if this were supported by two-thirds of the votes in the Danish Rigsdad and the
united Althing, and subsequently by 75 per cent of the votes
in a referendum in Iceland in which not less than 75 per cent of
those eligible voted. The Icelanders immediately declared their
intention of repudiating the Act of Union of 1918 at the first
opportunity. But for the Second World War, however, they
might well have failed to obtain all the necessary conditions.

On April 9, 1940, the Germans occupied Denmark. On the
following day, the Althing claimed the right to exercise all
those functions of government previously carried out on its
behalf by the Danes, on the grounds of Denmark's enforced
inability to fulfil its obligations under the agreements of 1918
and 1920. (A month later, the exercise of this freedom was somewhat curtailed by the British occupation of the island.) In
May 1941, this temporary measure was translated into a declaration that the continued inability of Denmark to carry out
its part of the Act of Union gave Iceland the right to sever all
ties with the Danish crown, and that it intended to exercise

this right at the first opportune moment. That moment was seized on February 25, 1944, when it became clear that the imminent liberation of Denmark and the return of constitutional government there threatened to destroy the grounds on which Iceland based its claim to independence. The necessary referendum was held in Iceland in May that year; 98·61 per cent of the electorate voted: allowing for discounted votes, 97·35 per cent for abolition of the Act of Union, 0·52 per cent against. At the same time, a new constitution of an Icelandic republic received 95·04 per cent of the votes; 1·44 per cent against. (For the text of the 1944 constitution, see Appendix 1.)

In the First World War, Iceland had been of moderate strategic importance but nevertheless remained in relative obscurity due, not only to its geographical isolation, but to the fact that it was for long of such minor military and commercial significance as to escape the conflicts which afflicted the sister countries of Europe through the centuries. Not until the invention of the steam trawler, the submarine and the aeroplane did Iceland acquire more than passing importance in the eyes of the Western world. By the outbreak of the Second World War, developments in the scale and sophistication of submarine warfare in particular made its fjords of vital significance to the warring powers of Britain and Germany. If German U-boats had been able to harass Britain's North Atlantic shipping lines from the safety of Icelandic waters, the war might have taken a different turn. It was for this reason that, on May 10, 1940, Britain occupied the island as a pre-emptive move to deny it to the Germans. Most Icelanders resented the manner of this occupation, but admitted its necessity as a logical consequence of their undoubted preference for British civilisation and occupation to that of Nazi Germany. A vociferous minority, mainly Communists still obedient to the Moscow line on 'German–Soviet friendship', denounced it as aggression, but the occupation was never seriously resisted and the rare wild shot in the dark at no one in particular was the only open manifestation of displeasure. Indeed, in April 1941, Iceland voluntarily became part of the sterling area. The duty of garrisoning Iceland was taken over by the United States on July 7, 1941, before America entered the war, in order to release British troops for service elsewhere. (An interesting situation might have arisen if American troops had had to repel an armed German invasion while they were still technically in the service of a non-belligerent nation.)

⊠

Until the union of Iceland and Norway under the Norwegian crown in 1262, the principal influences in Icelandic history were political, cultural and religious; but from the fourteenth century onwards, economic factors increased in significance, until, by the early Reformation period, they became important to the virtual exclusion of other considerations.

The early settlers, favoured by the climatic cycle then prevalent and with ample lands for their livestock, developed a relatively prosperous, if careless, agricultural economy which, supplemented by local fishing, gave them a fair standard of living and a modest surplus in the form of homespun for export in exchange for the commodities they lacked—among which timber featured prominently. Trade with Iceland was clearly profitable enough at the end of the thirteenth century for it to figure as a source of contention between the kings and prelates of Norway, who both wanted a share in it. Indeed, the union of 1262 stipulated that one of the conditions binding on the Norwegian king was the despatch of at least six ships a year with the necessary imports for Iceland. Control of this trade, however, was increasingly monopolised by non-Icelandic merchants and became a sensitive pressure-point on which the Norwegian kings played in their conflicts with their unsubservient Icelandic vassals.

During the Commonwealth period and in the early years of union, the structure of the Icelandic economy was instrumental in shaping the national character and attitudes. The farmer, usually working within easy distance of at least modest sea, or river, fishing opportunities, enjoyed an economic independence which was guarded jealously, and which accounts in part for the great store set by the luxury of personal honour.

Early in the fourteenth century, the Hanseatic merchants greatly extended their influence, despite resistance, throughout Norway and thus indirectly into Iceland. Their intervention critically altered the pattern of trade, for they did not want the traditional homespun but the now much-prized stockfish. The changing trade demands were also reflected among Iceland's other main trading partners, the English. In *The Libelle of Englyshe Polycye* (*c.* 1436) we read:

> Of Yselande to wryte is lytill nede,
> Save of stokfische: yet for sothe in dede
> Out of Bristowe, and costes many one,
> Men have practised by nedle and by stone
> Thiderwardes wythine a lytel whylle,
> Wythine xij yeres, and wythoute parille
> Gon and comen, as men were wonte of olde
> Of Scarborough under the costes colde.[2]

By this time, the trade with England was already well-established, notwithstanding the repeated attempts of the Danish kings to enforce their trade monopoly.

Edward III granted the citizens of Blakeney in Norfolk exemption from service to the crown on account of their trade with Iceland, a trade also carried out by the men of Lynn, although by about 1425 Bristol had become the centre of activity. In 1411, Eric of Pomerania, king of Denmark, Norway and Sweden, issued a proclamation prohibiting anyone from visiting the Icelandic part of his dominion without a special licence, but in the following year thirteen vessels were reported at one time fishing off a single stretch of the coast. Eric appealed in 1415 to Henry V to restrain his subjects from trading in defiance of the proclamation, and the English king complied with a rather half-hearted restriction excepting the usage of ancient times. The extent to which this was effective may be judged from the fact that, in 1419, as many as twenty-nine English ships were reported wrecked off the Icelandic coast during a storm. The illicit trade was actively encouraged by the Icelanders, who often themselves took part in it on the English vessels. With Denmark failing to supply its colony, the goods brought by the English and a few other unauthorised merchants represented a lifeline. The Icelanders' petitions to the Danish king went unheeded so they took matters into their own hands and were prepared to undertake considerable risks to obtain English goods, and in particular English beer. Thus, we find a paradox running through relations between England and Iceland over the centuries: while, in general, the English have behaved badly, intolerantly, greedily, even piratically, towards the Icelanders, they have also, time and again, however inadvertently, provided them with the means of economic survival and even of prosperity.

All attempts by the Danish authorities to curb or levy duties on English imports were thwarted by the ruthless and sometimes savage measures of the English merchants and fishermen which occasionally lost them even the respect of the local inhabitants favourably disposed to their illegal trading. The Vestmanna Isles, off the south coast (the 'Westmen's Isles', so-called after the ten Irish slaves who fled there after murdering the first settler, Leif), became virtually a colony from which the English fished and plundered as they pleased. The north coast suffered similar depredations, farms being regularly sacked and people held to ransom. In one instance, in the middle of the fifteenth century, the island's governor was taken, killed and his dismembered corpse returned as a gift to his wife. The reprisals taken by the Danish led, in 1469, to a brief, though hardly intense, war between Denmark and Britain. By the end of the fifteenth century, a treaty stated that 'English merchants and fishermen may freely repair to Tyle (Iceland) on paying the customary dues and getting their licences renewed annually': a formality which most of them continued to disregard. By the beginning of the sixteenth century, the English were back in force and as unruly as ever; so much so that, in 1518, King Christian of Denmark was on the point of selling the island to the English merchants and was only prevented from doing so by the loss of his own throne. It is tempting to speculate what might have been the consequences of the annexation of Iceland to the kingdom of England on the eve of its growth into the British Empire! Denmark and Britain were more seriously embroiled from 1801 to 1815 when, despite British attempts to alleviate the consequences of loss of trade, Iceland suffered even more severely than usual from the deprivation of the import of those few modest commodities necessary for its economy.

Although the English played a major part in these maritime activities, they were not alone. The German Hanseatic merchants we have already noted, and French vessels also came in considerable numbers both to fish and to raid until the end of the eighteenth century. Columbus is supposed to have visited Iceland in 1477, and perhaps found there the inspiration for his voyage to America. The unfortunate Icelanders even had several hundred of their inhabitants carried off into captivity in the early seventeenth century by Algerian pirates.

In 1602, the Danes imposed a complete trade monopoly excluding all but certain privileged Danish merchants from trade with the island. This, although never totally effective, contributed greatly to the steadily worsening poverty of the island in the seventeenth, eighteenth and early nineteenth centuries. Trade was extended to all Danish subjects only in 1777 and to foreigners in 1818. Gradually, throughout the nineteenth century, a slight improvement in living standards took place as a result of the increase in the fish trade. Not until the latter quarter of the century, however, did those changes begin to make themselves felt which were eventually to revolutionise the economy of Iceland.

In the nineteeenth century, two significant economic developments—one inspired, the other partly fortuitous—set Iceland again on the road to economic independence: the growth of the co-operative movement, and the great increase in the fish trade (for this latter see chapter 3).

The growth of the co-operative movement in Iceland must be without parallel in any other economically advanced state, but its lesson is perhaps most pertinent to the underdeveloped countries, for the co-operative movement began at a time when Iceland, too, was underdeveloped and found its trade almost entirely in the hands of a colonial power.[3] In 1855, only fifty-eight commercial concerns operated in Iceland, almost all of them foreign-owned. The farmers, still at that time the mainstay of the domestic economy and important exporters, by the very nature of their activities found themselves more and more deeply in debt to the merchants, who were mainly Danish. Their crying need was for credit on fair terms, but as long as foreign traders exercised their monopoly position to depress the prices paid to the farmers for their livestock (chiefly sheep), and inflate the prices of the necessities they purchased, there seemed no hope. Moreover, the economy as a whole suffered from the fact that foreign merchants came to Iceland, accumulated wealth rapidly, and then left the country taking their capital with them. This pattern was even followed by the one or two Icelanders who broke into private trade.

In 1844, the very year in which the weavers of Rochdale were unknowingly launching a world-wide movement, the first unsuccessful attempt at co-operative action was also being made in Iceland. But this setback did not end the story. The first co-operative society to be formed as a limited liability company was set up in Hunavátn in 1869. These early co-operators set forth their motives in forming their society in a document circulated throughout the island which marked the co-operative movement, not just as a commercial venture, but as a crucial factor in the growing Icelandic determination to reassert independence.

> In recent years the Danish merchants in this neighbourhood have behaved shamefully towards us, the people of Hunavátn county; not only have they themselves fixed the prices of foreign commodities sold to us and the goods we have delivered to them in exchange but, behaving like highway robbers, they give us more or less putrid and inferior commodities, such as grain mixed with worms, and many other similarly spoilt or adulterated foods, all of which they have sold to us as genuine and unspoilt commodities, having full knowledge of their inferior and detrimental quality.[4]

Thus from the outset of the movement, commercial exploitation through trade monopolies and dishonest dealing in trade practice were inseparably associated with the colonial power, whose citizens the merchants were. The implication throughout the whole of this document is that the one is the automatic consequence of the other.

The farmers of Husavík were another group being similarly exploited by the Danes, but they did not give up quite so easily as Gardar the Swede, the first to winter there, in 864. The farmers had been in the habit of driving their sheep over the mountains to Akureyrí, but it occurred to them to try to do business with a Scottish merchant, Slimon, whose vessels occasionally called at Husavík; and they wrote to him explaining their problem. In 1881, in response to their appeal, Slimon sent a ship to trade directly with the farmers of Husavík, but he told the local people that if he were to come again they would have to provide some kind of landing stage and a store. This the farmers duly did, forming a co-operative society for the purpose. The Scottish merchant continued to take the farmers' sheep and instead of paying cash, as he had at first done, brought goods for the people of Husavík. Their co-operative thus became both a producers' and a consumers' organisation: another unique feature of the co-operative movement in Iceland. As one local farmer, a leading member of the society, wrote in his diary: 'It was as if somebody had dropped a match into a pile of dry autumn leaves. People are beginning to think for themselves and to rely more on their own initiative and foresight and less on the providence of the high and mighty in the local places.'[5]

The incensed Danes were out for vengeance and waited only for the opportunity to destroy the upstart native co-operators. It came, as they thought, in the winter of 1867–68, when the north coast of Iceland lay in the paralysing grip of Arctic pack-ice more extensive and persistent even than usual during that decade. Örum and Wulff, the Danish firm which enjoyed the monopoly of trade in Husavík prior to the forming of the society, learned that the co-operative was running out of goods and refused to sell to society members, even for cash, or to sell to any farmer intending to part with his stock to the society. But Tönnes Wathne, a Norwegian captain then at Leith, touched by the plight of the co-operators, was eventually persuaded to attempt the hazardous voyage from the Firth of Forth to Husavík, which he reached in March, despite near-mutiny by a crew appalled at the dangers involved. Wathne wrote: 'The port is not very good, and the ship was in great danger; there was a strong gale blowing and the rough ice blocks drifted into the port; thus the unloading was hazardous. It was a hard job for the dockers to get the heavy sixteen-stone bags ashore because of the cold, fourteen degrees below zero centigrade. But all went well.'[6]

This marked a turning-point, for from then on all did go well with the Icelandic co-operatives and badly for the Danish merchants, who one by one were obliged to close down and sell out to their local competitors. The co-operatives were quick to adapt to changing market requirements. When, for example, in 1896 Britain felt obliged to restrict, virtually to ban, the import of live sheep through severe quarantine restriction imposed for fear of disease, the co-operatives soon moved into the field of freezing and storing carcass lamb.

Today the Co-operative Society, which is organised on a federal basis, is the largest single trading enterprise in Iceland and it claims that two-thirds of the population is affiliated to it. Dairies and slaughter houses, fishing vessels and processing plants, supermarkets and woollen-goods factories: there is virtually no part of the Icelandic economy in which the co-operatives do not play a major role. In 1959, for example, their turnover represented about an eighth of total gross national product.

There are many who would argue that the co-operative movement today, still closely identified with the Progressive Party, has too dominant a role in the economy. Others, co-operators, would insist that complete rural depopulation is averted only by the society's activities. But there can be no dispute about the movement's vital contribution to Iceland's economic, and hence eventual political, independence.

The total control of trade and transport by foreign powers had a number of effects on Iceland. It physically isolated all but a handful of its people, great travellers though they had once been, from the outside world at a time when conditions in Europe were changing rapidly. Moreover, it cut them off at a time when major cultural and linguistic changes, some might say corruptions, were taking place in the parent Scandinavian kingdoms. Whereas the Icelanders had once shared a common language with the Scandinavian homeland, they now found themselves almost unintelligible in the countries of their origin, and were consequently driven increasingly back on their own closed society.

But the most damaging effect was undoubtedly that occasioned by the changing trade-pattern on the Icelandic way of life. At a time when overgrazing and harsh winters were already putting a severe strain on a pastoral economy, the growth of the fishing trade was attracting ever-increasing numbers away from the land into the coastal villages. Men who had stood proudly on their ability to fend for themselves now depended for the necessities of life on their ability to purchase them from the proceeds of their sale of fish to foreign merchants. The control of their economic destiny, and with it to a great extent their political destiny, thus passed out of the hands of the Icelanders. They lost their independence when they lost that control, and regained it only when the chance of war turned the terms of fish trading dramatically in their favour.

3

If the Fish Should
Swim Away . . .

A GRAVEYARD of shrivelled skeletons oscillating gently with a
motion which sweeps an overwhelming stench towards you; a
forest whose disciplined leaves are dead fish; the upturned ribs of
a huge Viking ship planked with grey skin: in whatever metaphor
you may disguise it, there is no mistaking stockfish (cod) as it
hangs drying in the sun and wind. But it is seen less and less
often in Iceland now, and that delicacy of the Hanseatic trade
has played a steadily diminishing part in the country's economy
since the last quarter of the nineteenth century. Most of it
today is exported to West Africa; but, just as the Spanish Civil
War cost Iceland its major market for salted cod (saltfish) at a

critical time in the 1930s, so in our day the civil war in Nigeria and the expansion of the Ghanaian fishing industry threaten to reduce stockfish exports to Africa to a marginal economic activity. Fortunately, during the period of this commodity's decline, other forms of fishing and processing have been developed.

The first changes in the fishing industry came with changes in the nature of the fishing vessels themselves (Table 1 and note, p. 201). By the last quarter of the nineteenth century, second-hand decked sailing vessels, bought from a Europe which had turned to steam power, had replaced the old open rowing boats as the main fishing craft. The sailing vessels were themselves to disappear within another quarter of a century, in favour of the motor boats and trawlers which still form the Icelandic fishing fleet. The number of trawlers and motor boats increased steadily until the start of the First World War, when ten trawlers were sold off abroad as redundant. After the war, there was an almost desperate scramble for new trawlers, and the number of steam and motor vessels for line fishing also increased rapidly. The depression of the 1930s hit the Icelandic fishermen very hard, though, perhaps surprisingly, the number of motor boats over twelve tons continued to rise. By the outbreak of the Second World War, the trawler fleet had dropped from its peak of forty-seven to thirty-five; and wartime losses, which could not be replaced, reduced this to thirty-one. During the war, some of the older trawlers were taken out of 'mothballs' and used to ship fish on ice to Britain. In the post-war period, as after the First World War, the number of trawlers increased until the early 1960s,* when the change in the nature of the catch from whitefish (cod, halibut, plaice, haddock, etc.) to herring, due to the return to Icelandic waters of the more immediately profitable herring shoals, affected vessel-usage. Although trawlers cannot readily be adapted for herring fishing—for which the technique differs from the deep-sea trawl

* In 1963, there were forty-three trawlers in service. For development of the fishing fleet in this century, see Table 1, page 201 below.

for whitefish—the large motor vessels can soon switch from one catch to the other. During the post-war period, the number of ships of all sizes increased steadily, with a corresponding increase in those over 100 tons and a rise in the total tonnage. From 1952, when Iceland first extended its coastal fishing limits, there was a steady increase in the number of open motor boats and vessels under twelve tons: which suggests that the motives for restricting the activities of foreign vessels in the bays and fjords—the fish-breeding grounds—were, understandably, not entirely conservationist.

It is probably safe to say that the growth of the Icelandic fishing fleet has attained a plateau, measured in terms of tonnage and number of ships. If, as marine biologists have predicted, the limitations of the breeding capacity of the cod-grounds indicate that the actual tonnage caught cannot increase, and if the herring continue their unpredictable ways, then—until fish-farming arrives (and the Icelanders, of necessity, may be the first to introduce it)—the trend must be towards the more efficient use of capital invested in fishing rather than in an extension of the fleet. This means better equipment and better (and probably fewer) vessels, working even more intensively and for a longer season. The herring season, for example, has already lengthened from two or three months during the summer to the end of the year, but intensive fishing as a whole, largely because of weather conditions, lasts for only five or six months. The number of vessels fishing after December is only about a quarter of the number to be found fishing in May.

The productivity of the fishing industry is heavily dependent on two other factors: the equipment used for catching the fish, and its processing when caught. In the days of the small open boats and sailing vessels, fishing was by handline and dragnet. The best-quality fish used in the freezing industry is still caught by up-to-date versions of basically the same methods. The volume of the catch rose rapidly in the early part of this century with the introduction of the trawl, but it was

53

not really until the mid-1950s that the next revolutionary changes were made in the techniques of fish catching. Three of these dramatically combined to effect a complete shift in scale of operation.

The first grew from the tools of anti-submarine warfare. The sonar, or asdic (and, increasingly of recent years, radar) devices used to trace U-boats are now employed to track down the fish shoals with a scientific exactitude which has efficiently, if unromantically, superseded the skilled skipper's 'nose' for fish.

The second innovation was the use of the power block, due almost entirely to the persistence of one man, Ingvar Palmason, who chanced to see an early prototype in use on a Canadian ship. The old method of catching herring had been for the parent ship to lower two small boats which encircled the shoal before the net was closed by hand. The net was then laboriously manoeuvred to the side of the parent ship and the herring extricated: a slow and exhausting process, particularly in heavy weather. It was not until 1958 that the mass of Icelandic skippers was converted to the use of the power block by the great catch of one of their number. This skipper and his crew, impressed by Palmason's advocacy, had mastered the handling—and in particular, the location at the right point on the ship—of this high-pressure hydraulic system which uses the weight of the net itself to keep it close to the revolving pulley which drags it aboard.

At the same time that the power block made possible the handling of heavier and therefore larger nets, developments in the plastics industry made possible a new type of net manufactured from synthetic materials and almost twice as efficient in terms of weight for size. This was to lead to the third revolutionary change in fishing techniques. The problem of weight has always been a serious one for the safety of fishing vessels. The hazards of a ship's becoming top-heavy through too great a load of cumbersome deck-gear, particularly when every exposed part is rapidly icing up, have often been tragically demonstrated. But now, the old herring ship—probably under 100 tons, with a crew of between eighteen and twenty hands and fishing to a maximum depth of fifty fathoms with a four-ton net—could be replaced by a 300-tonner carrying twelve men and putting nets of eight to twelve tons' weight down to a depth of 100 fathoms.

The significance of this threefold revolution in fishing techniques can be gauged by the fact that, between 1955 and 1962, the increase in the Icelandic herring catch was of the order of 1,000 per cent.

It is no less significant, perhaps, that all these technical developments, although swiftly and efficiently deployed by Icelanders quick to see their advantages, have originated outside the country. Domestic critics of the way the Icelandic fishing industry is run argue that failure to invest now in research and development,* and inadequate manufacturing and repair industries serving the fishing industry, will be very dangerous to the national economy. If the size of the catch is to be inescapably limited by nature, then the means by which it is obtained and processed must become increasingly efficient if Iceland is to remain competitive in world markets and gain the full benefit of its exports. At present, Iceland imports over a million pounds' worth of fishing gear annually.

The processing of Icelandic fish has come a long way since a family laid its catch out to dry on the stones. The first important development, dating from about 1930, was the landing at British ports and markets of fish already iced on board the trawler. This trade increased quantitatively until the end of the Second World War, but as a proportion of the total catch only until 1940. The first small freezing plant was set up in the Vestmanna Isles in 1908, and the first factory for processing the surplus herring catch into meal for cattle began operating in 1911. For many years, neither of these activities played a

---

* Though in fairness it should be mentioned that research is, for example, now being carried out on the preservation of fish by irradiation.

particularly important role. The first great spur to their growth came during the depression of the 1930s, with the collapse of prices and the shrinking of the traditional markets for the older forms of fish exports. The second came during the war years 1939–45, with the insatiable demand of beleaguered Britain and the guaranteed prices of its Ministry of Food. It is well to remember that Iceland paid a very high price in human lives and vessels in meeting this wartime need. Yet it was this same need which accelerated the very great growth in fish freezing.[1]

Both shipping shortages and the 'emergency' market requirements of the British, whose meagre meat ration needed supplementing by fish, meant that fish had to be landed at British ports consistently in good condition throughout the year, not only during the short four- or five-month season of intensive fishing. The storage of fish over longer periods was necessary. This necessity gave a remarkable impetus to Iceland's hitherto insignificant fish-freezing and packaging industry during the war years which continued until the mid-1950s, when over half the whitefish catch was being frozen.* A decline set in after this; even so, during the next five-year period (1960–64), 48 per cent of the catch was frozen. In 1937, there were only fourteen freezing plants in Iceland, most of them rather small. By the middle of the war (1942), there were forty-four, and throughout the war they were being set up at the rate of seven or eight a year. Today there are some 100 freezing plants. However, with the decline of the frozen tonnage of whitefish, and even allowing for the growth in herring freezing, many of them are underutilised, with a consequent waste of the capital investment.

---

* Only 2 per cent of the cod catch in 1938 was frozen; but between 1940 and 1944, landings of frozen cod rose to 13·3 per cent (28,000 tons). A wartime necessity became a peacetime economic convenience. By the five-year period 1955–59, when Icelandic fish landings reached their peak, 55 per cent of the whitefish catch (202,000 tons) was being frozen, and of this cod represented approximately 60 per cent.

This underutilisation has been exacerbated by the rapid increase in the productivity of the freezing plants. (For example, the period 1961–65 saw a rise in productivity of approximately 30 per cent.) There were fortunes to be made in the boom in frozen fish during and after the war, for the process could double or treble the value of the catch (see Table 2, page 202). Plants for processing whitefish (and also herring) were set up without regard to the national requirements of the industry.

But at least the cod stays in one place. The same cannot be said of the fish that lays the golden eggs: the herring. Their ocean habitat varies widely in location off the Iceland coast. For example, the south-western coastal area which produced only 6·2 per cent of the total catch in 1946 brought in 70·3 per cent in 1950; yet by 1964 the herring catch here had fallen sharply to 16·5 per cent (see Table 3, page 202). One result of the migratory habits of the herring is the coastal necklace of unused or half-used plants built for converting herring into meal and oil, and of herring-salting stations.

The marketing of frozen whitefish has also shown a variegated pattern, with Britain and Continental and African nations being dramatically replaced in the early 1950s by the United States, and to a lesser extent the Soviet Union (see Table 4, page 202). In the later 1950s, Russia even surpassed the United States as a market; but in the 1960s Britain somewhat retrieved its position, while Russian purchases declined by almost half and those of other traditional markets disappeared almost completely. This left the United States as purchaser of over half of Iceland's frozen whitefish, largely from plants built by Iceland in the United States itself. The first freezing plant to be set up in the United States was at Nanticoke, Maryland, in 1956, when the Federation of Icelandic Freezing Plants Corporation—to which belong virtually all the plants not in the co-operative movement—set up the Coldwater Seafood Corporation to process and market Icelandic Fish in America.

57

The co-operatives themselves also entered the American market through an affiliated corporation which marketed the 'Samband' products. Both of these processing and marketing organisations are steadily expanding their business in the United States.

The decline in Britain's share of the frozen-fish exports was due to a combination of factors. The 1949 devaluation of the pound gave added incentives to British trawler owners. In any case, the British housewife was heartily sick of the boring packages of frozen fish dumped on her plate by the Ministry of Food throughout the war and presented in exactly the same form by an Icelandic fishing industry whose lack of imagination was encouraged by its government's subsidy system. Moreover, the devaluation of the krona in 1950 stimulated attention to the profitable and little-tapped American market. In addition, the trade with Russia, which had come to a complete halt in 1948 due to political differences arising from Iceland's decision to join NATO, was renewed in 1953; possibly as a manoeuvre to take advantage of the British trawler owners' 1952 ban on the landing of Icelandic fish, possibly as a natural consequence of de-Stalinisation in Russia. However, the Icelanders discovered that trading with the Soviet Union was not so easy an alternative as it seemed at first, for the USSR can take at least as ruthless an advantage of a small nation's economic necessity as any capitalist power.*

* Whether the Russians got the best that Iceland could offer is another matter; though it is probably an apocryphal story some Icelanders told me that when, during the 1950s, fish was sorted prior to processing, the sorters would put the best into cartons on their right, earmarked for the USA, and toss the poorer specimens into crates on their left, destined for the USSR. What is certainly true, and an amusing sidelight on trade with Russia, is that Soviet petroleum is marketed in Iceland by Western petrol firms. As usual, Russia stipulated the goods which Iceland might have in exchange for the roubles it earned. Of these, only petroleum and vehicles were of much use. While there has been a marked decline in the number of Russian

The trading switch in frozen fish to the United States has been due to Iceland's need to find relatively stable prices at as high a level as possible for its products. The setting up of factories in the United States, and the high-powered and skilled marketing of an excellent product, have secured for Iceland a strong position in the world's major consumer nation—although the potential embarrassment of such great dependence on one market should not be overlooked. Now that relations with Britain are good again, the Icelanders must be relieved to see a growing proportion of their frozen fish going to this traditionally strong market. Though Britain's share of frozen-fish exports in 1961–65 was only slightly more than half of what it had been in 1946–50, its improvement over the meagre figures of the fifties holds out to Iceland the hope of a broader distribution in its trade, with less dependence on one individual export market than in the past. Although the contribution of frozen fish to exports as a whole has declined since the high peak of the mid-fifties (cf. Table 12, page 208), it still plays a sufficiently large part for such considerations to be important.

The most lucrative part of the fishing industry is herring. But, unfortunately, catching herring is the most volatile of occupations. The herring shoals, in a rough calculation, seem to move in cycles of six or seven years at a time. We have already seen how greatly the catch has varied within and between the main fishing areas off the Icelandic coast. Were this the sole problem, it would present inconveniences but nothing more. However, in the lean years, the herring move far away from the coasts of Iceland and out of range of many of the herring boats. The size of the catch within a quinquennium can itself vary as much as by a factor of five (cf. Table 5,

---

cars to be seen on Iceland's roads, the petrol continues to flow through the marketing mechanism of the Western petrol giants, Esso, British Petroleum and Shell.

page 203). It is perhaps early to say, but by the end of 1967 it looked as if the herring catch was beginning to fail once more, heralding a new lean period for Iceland.

With herring, as with cod, the greater profit is to be derived from processing. Herring is salted and frozen for human consumption; oil is extracted for margarine and cooking fat, and the remnant is processed into meal for high-protein animal fodder. In 1964, 48·3 per cent of the total Icelandic fish catch of nearly one million tons was in the form of herring processed for meal and oil. By far the largest part goes into the meal process, and the Icelanders are now seeking ways of converting a greater proportion of their herring catch into the higher-price commodities for human direct or indirect consumption. The world demand for herring products, and particularly meal, continues to rise (annual consumption of meal went up between 1955 and 1965 from 1·25 to 3·4 million tons), but the prices in the world market have sunk rapidly in the last two years, due largely to the extensive production of the Peruvian fisheries.

There can be no doubt of the vast improvements in the efficiency of the Icelandic fishing industry, both before and after the catch is landed. The tonnage of the fleet rose only 14 per cent between 1960 and 1965, yet the catch increased 89 per cent. But two factors have eroded the advantages of this improved efficiency: domestic inflation, and fluctuating (recently falling) world prices. The 1964 catch was 64 per cent larger than that of 1960. In terms of dollars, this represented an increase in productivity of 75·5 per cent; but in terms of constant 1960 krona, it was an increase of only 33·6 per cent. Price-falls for herring products in recent years (the first half of 1967, for example) have been of the order of 30–40 per cent in a single year (see Tables 5 and 6 for catch and its utilisation). Such problems would be alarming enough for a fishing industry such as that of Britain, which plays a relatively small part in the national economy, and in any case works largely to supply the domestic market. For Iceland, the problems, as well as the latent opportunities, loomed far larger. The fishing and fish-processing industries account for approximately a quarter of Iceland's Gross National Product and for over 90 per cent of its exports, and employ one-sixth of the labour force. In 1880, 12 per cent of the population was engaged in the fishing industry; by 1940, this had risen to 20 per cent; but, with the substantial improvements in productivity, the proportion had fallen to 16·3 per cent by 1964.

In the fish-freezing plants and herring-sorting depots, the gay, vivacious and often very young girls, immaculately clean and hygienic in their aprons and caps, slice, cut and pack fish with an eye-deceiving dexterity which does not for a moment halt the flow of their ceaseless, frivolous, sometimes bawdily humorous conversation. How Icelandic women can talk! But generally one is so busy gazing raptly at them that it doesn't much matter, for one isn't listening. On the trawlers and fishing vessels, the tough and taciturn fishermen, drabbly dressed in blues and greys to match the sullen skies, hands like lumps of rope, faces like dried cod, eyes palely stripping all pretension from what they look at, go about their exacting and dangerous work. The ever-present danger in fishing in these northern waters is something to be borne in mind, for it is not just economic survival that depends on the sea but the fishermen's own physical survival too. When a man's work involves him in daily risking his life, he and his women folk are not likely to look kindly on man-made obstacles to winning a livelihood. One thing both these groups have in common: a capacity for hard work.

The extent of Iceland's dependence on its fish exports is expressed strikingly in the histogram. (For details of exports of major commodities, f.o.b., see Table 12, page 208.)

These figures must be seen in the context of Iceland's total economic situation. The country has very little in the way of indigenous raw materials and resources, other than hydro-electric and thermal power. Everything—from lavatory paper

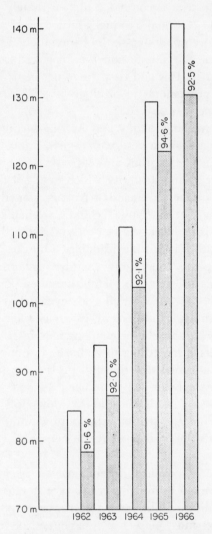

Icelandic fish exports as percentage of total exports (in million $)

to machinery, from screwdrivers to sou'westers—has to be imported. An English politician coined the political slogan, 'Export or Die'. Though this exaggerates the nevertheless basic problem of the British economy, it is virtually the absolute truth for Iceland.

During the first half of the sixties (1960–64), Iceland was fortunate in that the terms of trade moved strongly in its favour, to the tune of 23·4 per cent. This was principally due to a much more rapid rise in the prices paid for its fish products than the prices for such principal imports as vehicles, machinery, fuel, textiles and timber. But in the late sixties, Iceland faced a dilemma. As we have already seen, the pattern in the fishing industry suggests that the logical development is a more intensive use of capital, not only in the catching of fish, but also in the processing which it subsequently undergoes. However, the decrease of internal tariffs and increase of external ones in both the European Free Trade Association (EFTA) and the European Economic Community (EEC) were likely to make the export of Icelandic fish more difficult, for Iceland was a member of neither trade group.* Moreover, while the substantial export of fish in bulk to the United States does not meet with particularly high tariffs at the moment, the more fully processed the fish, the higher the tariff it must encounter. The general trade-pattern, therefore, would seem to be forcing on Iceland a reliance on the export of semi-processed fish rather than fully-processed fish products; and this is not in its best economic interest.

But an even more serious threat to Iceland's fishing industry began to appear in the latter half of 1968, when it was summed up for the writer by the present director of the Economic Institute in Reykjavík.

Our increasing worry is about trends so new that they hardly emerge in your writing or my article in the June (1968)

---

* Iceland's future relationship with the two communities is examined in chapter 6.

NATO Letter. It is that the Western nations will subsidise fishing so heavily that fisheries will suffer the same fate as agriculture, so that it will hardly be possible to specialise in and trade internationally in fish. Naturally, we can have no complaint about fishing being helped occasionally when it is a sick industry, or made to benefit from regional subsidies within reasonable limits. But news from a number of countries suggests that we may reap the catastrophic sum of uncoördinated decisions by individual nations to subsidise on a massive scale without regard to the resulting over-all fishing effort or supply on the market. When the economic adviser asks for policy confrontation with the others, people shrug their shoulders and say 'the British are not on talking terms with us'. This policy of subsidisation is all the more serious in that it is added to ruthless expansion in the planned economies and the natural tendency of low-income countries to push old, and ever newer, rafts afloat and get the fish themselves.[2]

The extent of their dependence on fish exports makes Icelanders sensitive, even selfish, where their fishing interests are concerned and much conditions their attitude to matters relating to the international control of fishing and territorial waters—as we shall see when we come to examine the 'cod war' in chapter 6. But Iceland has adopted a far from negative attitude to this basic economic problem and is not content just to cry 'not fair' whenever its capacity to earn a livelihood solely from fishing is threatened. In the next chapter we shall see that the government is making strenuous efforts to diversify the economy and that the difficulties it faces in so doing are daunting indeed.

4

The Search for Economic Security

BJARNI BENEDIKSSON, prime minister of Iceland, smilingly admits that the past success of his government may have depended as much on the vagaries of the migratory herring as on its own efforts. The fact that a few days before our interview (June 1967) his Independence party had just been returned to office for another four years did little to relieve his anxieties. As he put it: 'It's an unstable foundation for a state, to build upon herring in the sea which may quickly swim away.' During our conversation, he repeatedly expressed his determination to do his best to diminish this element of uncertainty by means of diversification of the Icelandic economy. But the problems are formidable, and several of the possible partial solutions themselves entail other economic difficulties. On the

65

other hand, the fortunes of war and nature have bestowed some economic advantages, particularly in the field of capital formation.

An analysis of Icelandic imports shows the difficulty, in view of the almost total lack of natural resources, of either replacing imports by domestic production or of expanding exports sufficiently to give a safety margin on the import bill (see Table 13, page 209). Yet failure to overcome at least one, and preferably both, of these sets of difficulties threatens to imperil Iceland's extremely high standard of living—probably today the highest in Europe. The seriousness of the problem is obvious when one realises that, in recent years, the value of imports has been consistently greater than the value of exports. Any economic diversification in Iceland must be based either on raw materials and power, or on brains and human skills.

❁

Although it lags far behind the fisheries in export value, Iceland's second major natural resource, so far at least, has been its agriculture. Little has changed on the Icelandic farm over the centuries except perhaps the farmhouse. In place of the old long house of the early settlers or the primitive turf and stone dwelling of the years of poverty, a simple but comfortable concrete home, with its gay green or red roof marking it out like a lonely homing beacon, houses the family. But the farm still stands in isolation from its neighbours, more on the English than the continental village pattern. Life still revolves around the hay crop to be gathered from the meadows for the sheep, and from the home field (or *tun*) about the farm for the cattle. The scattered pastures often stretch far into the distant lava fields and along the river banks in sparse lonely patches from which the sheep have to be retrieved each autumn.

Although, as in settler times, cattle represent a greater (by 25 per cent) proportion of farm produce by value, it is the far more numerous sheep which shape the character of Icelandic

66

farms.* If there is machine-shearing instead of hand-clipping, if the hay to feed the sheep is mown by power-cutter instead of hand-scythe and the bales towed by tractor and trailer rather than carried on either side of an Icelandic pony, the differences are essentially superficial ones of technique. Not that the new methods and standards are unwelcome; the centrally heated farmhouse, the liberal fare, the car in the garage, would not be readily exchanged for poverty; and Icelandic farmers are well aware that it is easier to maintain a dignified independence when you are prosperous.

The modern Icelandic farmers enjoy even greater independence than their forebears. The great majority of them today are freehold owners of their farms, whereas in the middle of the nineteenth century most were tenant farmers, freeholders forming only 17 per cent of the total. About one-fifth of the Icelandic farms are owned by Church or State, and most of these have a system of family tenancy whereby the lease automatically passes from father to one parentally designated son. The government has encouraged, even over-encouraged, the farmer to increase his output, primarily by means of heavy consumer subsidies, but also by export subsidies, limited to 10 per cent of agricultural produce, and investment incentives. While farm incomes have been boosted in this way from motives of social egalitarianism, the system has resulted in very high capital investment in an area already uncompetitive as an export field. Those wishing to take up farming are encouraged to do so by a generous system of government grants and loans. Nevertheless, the number of private farms has remained about 5,500 for some six years, while estates farmed by tenants have declined from 5,100 in 1960 to 4,850 in 1966. The number of those persuaded by financial inducements to take up farming is offset by those leaving the land for Reykjavík, many of whom sell their holdings to neighbouring farmers. This trend was

* An all-time high of 850,000 sheep was reached in 1967, but cattle had fallen from a peak of 60,000 in 1965 to 54,000 by 1967.

very marked in the early 1950s when the ravages of a sheep disease, which had already made its presence felt before the war, reduced the number of sheep by more than half.

But, despite the growth in domestic consumption due to rapid expansion in the population, the saturation of the home market and the steady decline of agriculture's share of the export trade (from 7 per cent in 1962 to 3·8 per cent in 1965) have probably set a ceiling on agricultural production which has almost been reached. It has risen by only 7·1 per cent in the period 1961–67. For all its barrenness, and despite the destruction of much productive land over the centuries, Iceland is still a country with too few farmers chasing too much land. With the enduring problem of transport costs overseas, there is little scope for expansion in heavy and bulky agricultural exports, chiefly mutton and butter.

Food is, in fact, a major Icelandic import; so that butter, milk and, perhaps surprisingly, bread are the only foodstuffs which can be bought in Iceland at roughly their British price. But the average Icelandic family eats, and drinks, extraordinarily well from a wide range of Continental and American dried, canned and pre-packed foods. Its own specialities—the yoghurt-like *skyr*, shark meat, smoked mutton and lamb, fat trout and exotically spiced and prepared salmon—would not offer, delicious as they are, sufficient variety, and Icelanders would have a dull diet indeed if thrown back on their own resources. Although there is little risk, whatever world circumstances, of their going hungry, they are greatly dependent on imported cereals, since there is an almost total absence of home-grown cereals (only a few hundred experimental acres of struggling oats, barley and rye). Any disruption in cereal imports would be a blow to a people so given to the consumption of cakes and biscuits.* Deprivation of coffee would probably drive them mad. They are the world's most intensive consumers of coffee; they

---

* Prices on the home market for these and other foodstuffs are fixed by a government-sponsored committee of producers and consumers.

brew it strong, black and aperient on every possible occasion, and a few impossible ones.

The farmers in different districts have a number of peripheral activities, chief among which seems to be riding the sturdy little Icelandic ponies—once much used as pit-ponies in Britain— which can be seen moving swiftly if to little purpose after the tough and scraggy-looking sheep on the hillsides or browsing in indolent and charming hundreds by the edge of the road. With their own peculiar ground-consuming gait, the *tölt*, half-way between a walk and a trot, they traverse country of all kinds, no matter how rough, with a seemingly hydroelastic suspension system which gives the lucky rider the impression he is on a hovercraft, so little undulation does he feel. Riding these ponies, of which there are almost as many (approximately 40,000) as there are cattle, is one of the Icelander's principal pleasures, and during the summer you may see more than a thousand ponies and their owners gathered for a meet where sport and business, horse-talk and literary criticism, whisky and wenching are the order of the twenty-four-hour day.

In the coastal areas, the farmers catch the cliff-nesting birds, in particular the puffins. This looks a dangerous way of adding to the family income, for the farmer scales down a sheer cliff at the end of a rope, netting the frightened birds as they rise from their nest. Its appeal is as much sporting as commercial. To see one of these cliff-hunters is to be reminded of the scene in *King Lear* when Edgar pretends to lead the blinded, suicide-bent Gloucester to the cliff-top and describes the imagined abyss below:

> The crows and choughs that wing the midway air
> Show scarce so close as beetles: halfway down
> Hangs one that gathers samphire, dreadful trade!
> Methinks he seems no bigger than his head:
> The fishermen that walk upon the beach
> Appear like mice. . . .

A much more profitable use of the island's wild fowl is enjoyed by those farmers lucky enough to have, and encourage, a colony of eider-duck on their land. The breast-fluff from the plain female birds, so cleverly camouflaged that you are in danger of stepping on them in their marshland nests, goes to make the famous eiderdown and fetches £30 a kilo. The duck makes its nest by plucking the down from its breast for lining and covering the delicately pale green eggs. The skill in eider-duck farming is to take just sufficient down from the nest to encourage the female duck (the male by contrast is a flamboyant blend of black, green, brown and white) to replenish it without taking so much that she gives up in despair and abandons the eggs. Of conventional poultry you will see very little—the total poultry population is approximately 98,000—but Iceland is self-sufficient in eggs and table birds.

There may perhaps be near the farm, particularly in the areas of sandier soil, a small crop of potatoes or swedes; no other root vegetables or fruit can survive the climate. The most spectacular fringe activity is undoubtedly the small hot-house industry which has sprung up since 1923 in glasshouses heated by the steam and hot water that pours so abundantly from the ground throughout the island. The biggest of these developments is at Hveragerthi, some thirty-five miles from Reykjavík, where in winter there is the dramatic contrast of a snow-covered landscape and rows upon rows of bunches of huge (and rather tasteless) bananas under glass. An even more striking contrast is set by the flowers and tomatoes which are the more usual product of the greenhouses. It is perhaps typical of the Icelanders that, no sooner had they discovered and developed a new means of producing things hitherto beyond their reach, than they devoted a substantial part of its output to the aesthetic, counting the growing of flowers as important as the growing of food.

Despite the fact that life on a modern Icelandic farm, however bleakly situated, is nearly always comfortable and prosperous—although like farmers the world over, the Icelanders will not often admit this—rural depopulation and the increasing difficulty in maintaining viable communities throughout the island are major problems.

At the turn of the century, 80 per cent of the working population was involved in agriculture; in 1930, it was 40 per cent; today it is less than 14 per cent. This much smaller number of farmers produces far more than their forebears ever did. Aided by mechanisation, by nitrogen fertilisers from a government plant set up in 1954, by sophisticated processing industries, by carefully controlled and sustained market prices, things seem much easier for the farmer and in a practical sense they are.

❊

The most formidable threat to an evenly balanced distribution of population has been the growth of Reykjavík. Yet the development of a sophisticated technological society depends on the interplay of skills and activities of a large number of people necessarily concentrated in a single place.

Coincidentally the place of the first permanent settlement, subsequently the centre of such Danish authority as was exercised, Reykjavík, until even the end of the nineteenth century, was little more than a village. The turn in its fortunes, imperceptible at the time, probably came in 1752 with the start of a woollen manufactory for which the Danes had granted a licence. It was not a commercial success in the face of the Danish competition, but it established a precedent and marked Reykjavík as the focus for commercial expansion. In 1806, the capital had only 446 inhabitants, of whom twenty-seven were in jail. By 1860, the population had risen to but 700, approximately one-seventieth of the total population of the island. An English traveller in the early 1850s, the Reverend J. E. Cross, described it thus:

Poor, lonely Reykjavík! It is indeed a cold, arctic-looking capital! The struggle for existence against the uncongenial

71

climate is most evident, even in the architecture of the place. All looks poor and grim. A small village of Swiss chalets is perhaps the closest counterpart of it in our latitudes, but even such a village would be a formidable rival to the capital of Iceland. The best houses, those of the Danish merchants, are indeed comfortable enough within, but the general look of the place is dreary and most dispiriting. The larger houses are built altogether of wood imported from Denmark and Norway, while the cottagers' poor huts are massive stone to the square. This seems extraordinary, but we are told that the wooden structure is by far the more warm and comfortable. A few broad, half-built streets of such houses as these, a Lutheran Church of some pretensions, a good size building called the College and a solitary windmill, a dreary stagnant lake or pool as a background, flanked by a few dreary fields. Imagine this, and the metropolis is before you.[1]

Today the world's most northerly capital, Reykjavík is also one of its most striking. If you arrive by air, your first glimpse is of a toytown: a gallimaufry of roofs, bright red, green, grey, purple; and then suddenly you seem to be plunging down into the very midst of them, for the smaller airport (there is a larger one twenty miles away in Keflavík) is tucked away in part of the city itself. But, once into the city, the toytown image vanishes with the metropolitan bustle. Everywhere is evidence of an almost febrile prosperity: shops crammed with goods; jostling pavements of urban-hurrying citizens; a peaky little blonde, eight years old, candyfloss in one hand, a bundle of copies of the evening paper, *Visir*, under the other arm, and a raucous penetrating shout of her wares; dancehalls, restaurants, mini-skyscrapers and mini-skirts. This is modern Reykjavík. Here, and in the outlying network of suburbs, live almost 100,000 people, more than half the population of Iceland: a busy, thriving vortex, sucking into itself too much of the life which ought to sustain it and serve as its base. Soon perhaps it will be choked with its own success and die.

Reykjavík is a topheavy, miniaturised city, not in the stature of its buildings, but in its activities. A city which might be a provincial centre or university town elsewhere in Europe staggers under the weighty growth of all the great organisms of a modern state and their attendant bureaucracy. Yet each, when examined closely, is only a handful of men occupying a floor or two of a modern office block. Everywhere shops and services seem to proliferate to meet the needs of the capital's citizens; the five newspaper offices in place of the local evening paper, the university, the technical and nautical colleges, libraries, theatres, law courts, offices of the corporations and societies, the free-enterprise import merchants handling everything from paper clips to bedroom furniture, the motor showrooms and tourist offices and innumerable public swimming pools—all is activity but with productivity hard to discern. If you do come across a 'factory', it will be a small engineering works or garage employing a handful of men, a father-and-son carpentry business or a modest building company. For industry on any scale commensurate with the dignity of a capital city you must go down to the harbour. There you will see serried ranks of tough little fishing vessels, gag at the ripe smell of gutted fish and leaking diesel oil, shiver in the subhuman temperatures of the deep-freeze stores, and dodge the cranes unloading the passenger-cargo ship at the main quay. Only really in the harbour does Reykjavík, for all its charm and cleanliness, cease to be a homunculoid town and become a city.

With urbanisation come, albeit in a milder form than elsewhere, all the attendant social problems: family instability, juvenile delinquency, and so on. Only two factors prevent the draining away of the rural population from being complete: the development of modern transport and communications, and the recognition by the government, as by its predecessors, of the need for positive action to redress the imbalance, to encourage

73

the disproportionate growth of facilities and amenities in the rural centres before it is too late. For centuries, the essence of life in Iceland has been conditioned by habitation in a series of small scattered communities, bound together by esoteric, abstract things, by a kind of social and cultural telepathy of common origin rather than by physical confrontation. Then, over three short decades, came a sudden concentration of population in one centre. The impact of this on a people conditioned for so long to a wholly different form of life was traumatic. It is symptomatic, perhaps, that it is precisely where there has been the greatest concentration of people that the co-operative movement, with its emphasis on voluntary communal effort, has made least headway.

⊗

In sharp contrast with Reykjavík, there are in the western fjords today fewer people than there have probably been at any time in the nation's history: just a little over 10,000. Certainly, a look at the population figures of recent years shows that the trend, until 1965 at least, had been halted. People were not only staying; some were coming back; and, although there was still a net outflow, a balance had almost been attained. How-

Population of Westfjord District, 1940–67*

	1940	*1950*	*1960*	*1965*	*1967*
Barthastrand (county)	2,276	1,752	1,679	1,536	1,499
Patricksfjord	721	858	829	1,007	1,019
Isafjord	2,833	2,808	2,725	2,696	2,704
Isafjord (county)	5,041	3,840	3,698	3,711	3,718
Stranda (county)	2,082	1,908	1,576	1,485	1,375
Totals	12,953	11,166	10,507	10,435	10,315
Average yearly fall from previous census	—	178·7	65·9	14·4	60

* *Source:* Statistical Bureau of Iceland. The 1967 figures are provisional, as estimated at December 1, 1967.

ever, provisional figures for 1967 (which became available only after my visit to the area) show a resumption of the exodus which may or may not be temporary; the time-span is too short to tell.

Högni Torfasson is a good example of the men who are prepared to make something of the north-west. He lives in its largest town, Isafjord; its population, 2,700, is over a quarter of the region's total. Like so many Icelanders, he has two jobs. He is editor of the local weekly paper (it sells a phenomenal 2,000 copies each issue; there can scarcely be an adult in the area who doesn't read it), and organiser for the Independence party. Naturally, he claims that the government of which his party is the dominant partner has achieved wonders, but he does have some hard facts to back him. He described* the people in his area as being, a few years ago, 'fretful', always grumbling that the government never did anything for them. Now, 'they have a renewed faith in their community'.

The cost of living is certainly higher in the north-west, with goods bearing the additional transport costs; but, on the other hand, taxes are lower, coming to only 60 per cent of the metropolitan total. The basic problem is that if you do not work in the fishing industry, you do not work at all; and this, with the ever-rising standards of education of an already highly educated people, is a source of great discontent to the young. The only other industrial employment in Isafjord is a factory making double-glazed windows and employing about thirty people. The change in the psychology of the region came about in 1965, when the Icelandic government received a loan of $2 million from the Council of Europe's resettlement fund. Matching it with a similar investment, the government embarked on an ambitious development programme, principally of improved communications by road within the province. The local people could at last see concrete evidence of government

---

* In an interview with the author in 1967; but see also the results of the 1968 presidential election described on page 109.

concern. The present government favours the policy of dispensing benefits as widely as possible throughout the provinces.

Another school of thought in the rural depopulation controversy is represented by Bjarni Einarsson, the young and vigorous mayor of Akureyrí, the capital of the north, who was formerly a member of the Economic Institute in Reykjavík which moulds so much government policy. He argues—with vested interest, admittedly, but with much logic—that the only effective way to counter the pull of Reykjavík is to create a centre in the north no less magnetically attractive. He is bent on making Akureyrí, just such a centre. He feels that the counter-attraction must be centred on a place, a second city, carrying authority and offering a full range of governmental and social services without unnecessary duplication. The country's population is too small to allow of this being done effectively in more than one place other than the capital; as the leading growth point and already the second largest centre (population 10,000), Akureyrí is the natural choice. Bjarni is concentrating, therefore, on improving the efficiency of the city management, of making it planning-conscious. He is anxious to attract firms to Akureyrí—where the KEA (the local co-op) is by far the largest, indeed almost the only, large employer, with 550 people on its payroll. He does not mind even if these firms are foreign. Direct trade with Akureyrí for foreign imports is another policy intended to reduce the cost of living; and an industrial training centre is being set up to improve local skills.

The pattern he sees for the future is of a few specialised fishing villages and fewer and much larger farms, all looking to the city as a service centre. If the change in the over-all pattern of Icelandic life is accepted as total, desirable and inevitable, then this certainly seems one good way to bring about the change under controlled conditions. But, then Akureyrí is a stronghold of the Progressive party, which at the time of writing (February 1969) is in opposition and not therefore likely to attract government support on the necessary scale. One astonishing factor, given a government commitment to redressing the imbalance by developing the rural areas, is the absence of any form of investment grants or tax incentives to companies willing to set up factories and offices in these regions. The strongest safeguard against complete rural depopulation, however, is probably the simple fact that fishing, the mainstay of the economy, itself requires a peripheral distribution of harbours, processing plants and other resources.

But whatever the differences, political and economic, between Högni Torfasson and Bjarni Einarsson, they are both agreed on one thing: the key to any successful development outside the south-west is improved communications.

※

It is difficult for an outsider to appreciate just how appalling communications were in a country fragmented by swift, bridgeless rivers, encysted by a huge central desert and ringed by dangerous seas. Bjarni's father, for example, in the first two decades of this century, thought nothing of walking 230 kilometres in five days to catch the ship to Akureyrí, to arrive a month late for school. The postman would come once a month on horseback, and news, by the time it reached the east, was six weeks old. Today, there are dirt roads to even the remotest parts of the island, and Iceland has more miles of road per person than any other country. One person in six has a motor car, and buses and lorries are plentiful. There is a radio in every house and a telephone in most or within reasonable distance. But off the main circuit from Akureyrí to Reykjavík on through the south-west to Keflavík and Vík, the roads—although constantly attended by scrapers and bulldozers—are often sorry, pitted, lava-strewn affairs, blocked for much of the year by snow or mud.

The real prime mover, of people at least, in Iceland is the aeroplane. There are a host of light aircraft (ranging from Piper Comanches to Cessnas and Fokker Friendships)—for internal

77

flights by Iceland Air and half-a-dozen small private companies. Iceland Air also runs frequent services to Western Europe, as does the international airline, Loftleider, which also covers the North Atlantic. There are over seventy registered airfields, and many unregistered ones. However, the amenities of these airfields must not be exaggerated. Often the only thing to tell you that you have reached one is two parallel lines of brightly painted yellow or orange boulders, between which the terrain looks a trifle smoother than elsewhere. The strip may be in mid-desert or hacked out of the side of a narrow fjord. But Icelandic pilots are incredibly skilful and the internal routes are used to such an extent in virtually all weathers that every year over three-fifths of the Icelandic people go somewhere by plane, often at subsidised prices.*

The hope is that the development of means of communications of all kinds, by giving both remote and direct contact with centres of population, will make people willing to remain in the isolated districts as much as necessary. The degree of that necessity, in a country with surplus agricultural production is, as we have seen, a matter of debate. It is not impossible that there could come some point (indefinable as yet, admittedly) at which the balance would be fatally disturbed between physically concentrated societies, such as Reykjavík, and harmoniously but tenuously connected societies in the rural parts of the island, so that the nation would no longer have that leven of independence, of intellectual and imaginative vigour cultivated in solitude and isolation, which makes Icelanders Icelanders.

The improvement in communications is clearly essential to the development of tourism, potentially a large foreign-exchange earner. Iceland's location, coupled with its bizarre and wonderful landscape, offers an ideal outlet for those seeking unusual holidays off the beaten track. At present, although there

* Iceland would certainly appear to be a country in which the use of small hovercraft in bad weather seasons could be profitably developed.

are very good hotels in Reykjavík and a few in the provinces, holidaying in Iceland in comfort is an extremely expensive business—although it costs surprisingly little to get there. The devaluations of the krona of November 1967 and November 1968 may eventually help, but the great majority of tourists to Iceland today are young people travelling cheap, roughing it and bringing their own supplies. For these, Iceland presents a marvellous opportunity for adventure and aesthetic experience, and the school houses thrown open for little or no charge during the summer provide far greater comfort than the youth hostels of Europe, to which most of them are accustomed. Clearly, Iceland should continue to encourage them for they will be good friends for the future.

The important economic consideration, however, must be to attract the moderately prosperous tourist rather than the very wealthy now found at the other end of the spectrum of visitors to the island. A good distribution of hotels at the key scenic spots in the country, subsidised if necessary to bring them within the European middle-class expenditure bracket; more comfortable transport facilities; greater use of the fact that Iceland is in the sterling area, especially when foreign–exchange limits are imposed on the British—development on these lines could all boost a valuable industry, Not that considerable advances have not been made, the most significant of which is the twenty-four-hour and forty-eight-hour stop-over tour on transatlantic flights. The yearly flow of visitors of all kinds amounts to nearly a quarter of the population. The revenue from tourism, including fares and freight charges by sea and air, brings in 71 per cent of Iceland's invisible earnings.

⌘

Location and scenery, fish and grass are not an overwhelming range of nature's bounties on which to build a sophisticated economy. For a few years in the last century, sulphur was mined, but it is no longer economically exploitable. There are

79

only two other raw materials to be found in Iceland today: the ingredients for cement, and diatomite.*

With the lack of timber and steel, and the very high cost of importing them, Reykjavík might still look rather as the Reverend Cross described it but for the indigenous supply of materials for making concrete. Volcanic pumice is an important ingredient, particularly for certain kinds of cement, and some is exported to Europe. But the apparent total absence of limestone appeared to present an insuperable obstacle to making cement, and hence concrete. Then the Icelanders had the brilliant idea of dredging up from the sea bed the great limerich layer of seashells deposited over the millennia. Thus there flourishes a few miles from Reykjavík a cement industry with an annual output of 100,000 tons, quite adequate for Iceland's present needs.

The discovery of the location of diatomaceous soil in Iceland was the result of painstaking research by Icelandic and German geologists, and there now exists a small extraction plant near Lake Myvátn which will soon be earning useful foreign exchange from exports to the world's pharmaceutical, brewing and other industries needing high-quality diatomite filtres.

Nature has provided Iceland with one other natural resource of value in the modern world: power. Its importance to Iceland's future was predicted as long ago as 1832 by the English mathematician and engineer, Charles Babbage† who wrote:

> In Iceland, the sources of heat are still more plentiful; and their proximity to large masses of ice seems almost to point

* This substance, originally used in the manufacture of dynamite, consists of the silicaceous part of the millennial deposits of a dead, minute unicellular algae in certain geological strata.

† Graduating from Peterhouse, Cambridge, in 1814, and a Fellow of the Royal Society at the age of twenty-four, Babbage built the earliest automatic calculating machine, invented the ophthalmoscope, and devised in 1827 the table of logarithms. In his later years, he was chiefly known for his fierce hostility to organ-grinders.

out the future destiny of that island. The ice of its glaciers may enable its inhabitants to liquefy the gases with the least expenditure of mechanical force; and the heat of its volcanoes may supply the power necessary for their condensation. Thus, in a future age, power may become the staple commodity of the Icelanders, and of the inhabitants of other volcanic districts; and possibly the very process by which they will procure this article of exchange for the luxuries of happier climates, may in some measure tame the tremendous element which occasionally devastates their provinces.[2]

It is estimated that the rivers and waterfalls of the country represent a reserve generating capacity of no less than 35 thousand million kilowatts per annum. On top of this must be counted the considerable power to be derived from geothermal activity. The constant high-pressure steam jets, already tapped and controlled in some parts of the island, can be quite easily harnessed to generate electricity, particularly for local use. Electric power, if it can be offered cheaply enough, is a saleable commodity even far from the main centres of industry and raw materials. The development of the giant ore-carriers (40,000 tons and over) has made it sound economic sense—as the Ghanaians are finding with the Volta river dam—to ship raw materials, such as bauxite and alumina, to a distant source of power for smelting and processing. Just such an aluminium-smelting project at Burfell—jointly financed by American bonds, a loan from the International Bank for Reconstruction and Development, and Icelandic governmental and private funds—is now in hand; when completed, it will be the biggest single foreign-exchange earner after the fishing industry, as well as providing surplus power for a rapid expansion of domestic industries. In May 1965, the Althing created the National Power Company, jointly owned by the state and the city of Reykjavík, to undertake the construction on the Thjorsa river, sixty-three miles east of the capital, of a hydroelectric power-generating station. It will provide sufficient electricity for south-west Iceland from 1969 to the end of 1975, as well as for the aluminium-smelting plant to be built at Burfell.

The Burfell project is a run-of-river plant with six 35,000 kw generating units. The first three of these and the service facilities for the remaining generators, on which work started in 1966, will be in operation by mid-1969 to coincide with the starting up of the first 'pot-line' of the smelter with an estimated output of 30,000 tons of aluminium per year and absorbing 60,000 kilowatts. The second half of the project will be in operation by 1975, bringing the aluminium output to 60,000 tons and the extra generating capacity for south-west Iceland to 90,000 kilowatts. As part of the total system, there will be a water storage development at Lake Thorisvátn to wash away ice past the Thjorsa diversion and to sustain the flow of the river which, however, usually exceeds the demands of the generating plant.

It is estimated that the Burfell project will cost $43·2 million while the first stage of the Straumsvík smelter will cost $35 million. (All figures cited in this context are at 1965 prices.) When the first stage of the project is operational it will earn $15 million in foreign exchange and this will eventually rise to $35 million.* Interest, profits, imported services and raw materials have to be paid for in foreign exchange, but nevertheless the over-all operation will represent a very substantial contribution to Iceland's balance of payments. Moreover, the Swiss company has guaranteed the Icelandic government a foreign-exchange surplus at all stages of the operation. In local terms, the construction work on the project represents a labour-demand just at a time when economic recession has, for the first time in many years, resulted in spare manpower in Iceland.

---

* The Schweizerische Aluminium AG has entered into an agreement with the government which guarantees minimum yearly foreign exchange earnings of $1·35 million from 1969 to 1972, and $2·25 million from then until the contract expires in 1994. This excludes the sale of power to the smelter.

While the government properly takes pride in maintaining Iceland's full, indeed overfull, level of employment, some economists might argue that Iceland needs some surplus labour as a means of reducing the inflationary pressures. When the Burfell project is complete, it will employ between 300 and 500 men. One per cent of the present labour force will thus be involved in adding an estimated 3 per cent to the GNP.

Already the stimulus given, not just to the national economy but to regional activity, by the Burfell project can be detected, and it is worth noting that the Thjorsa river scheme is far from the largest potential power-generating scheme in Iceland. This is probably at Dettifoss near Myvátn in the north (a little less than sixty miles from Akureyrí). A major hydroelectric development here, with the associated large-scale industry, would be invaluable in redressing the economic imbalance between north and south-west. Perhaps the Icelandic government should put out feelers to those aluminium companies growing increasingly impatient with the British government's inability to make up its mind about locations of power sources for the plant scheduled to be set up in Scotland only 800 or so miles away.

One other asset which the Icelanders possess and which should not be overlooked in gauging their economic resources is brains. Small as the population is, its potential for reaching a very high level of technical skill is great. Just as Switzerland, admittedly by no means so deprived by nature, has profitably specialised in finance and small-scale precision engineering, so might Iceland seek similar fields. It needs to develop industries in which intelligence and dexterity are the principal ingredients, where neither the raw materials nor the finished product are excessively bulky, however expensive. Electronics, particularly perhaps computers, and communications systems, petrochemicals and plastics are industrial fields which Iceland's economic planners could profitably consider.

The Icelanders have already undertaken a number of bucca-neering, if sometimes rather improvident, commercial ventures with a verve which promises well for further attempts at diversification. The development of Loftleider exemplifies this spirit. In 1950, one of Loftleider's rather decrepit DC3s, carrying a bizarre cargo of industrial diamonds, performing dogs and a dead American WAC colonel, crashed and apparently disappeared. Five days later, when the search had been abandoned, a trawler picked up an SOS which located the aircraft in the middle of Vatnajökull, Iceland's largest and highest glacier. With a characteristic touch of generosity and bravado, the locally stationed American air force offered to go to the rescue. Its ski-fitted C-47 came swiftly and ignominiously to grief, was unable to take off and had to be abandoned as a total loss.

Once the Icelanders had rescued both crews, the Loftleider managers worried away at the tempting prospect of retrieving the American aircraft; their own was fit only for scrap. The first step was to buy it from the disbelieving Americans, for the princely sum of $700. Doggedly and methodically, the salvage team worked on foot and with snow tractors, enduring incredible hazards, to move the aircraft nearly sixty miles to a lower valley where the engines would work again and where the wheels beneath the skis did not penetrate the frozen crust of snow on the landing strip which had been prepared. The Icelanders were eventually successful, and with the $80,000 paid them by a Spanish airline which bought the C-47, they launched the first of a fleet of modern aircraft.

Even this boost could not sustain the new company, which in 1952 and 1953 found its trading losses threatening liquidation. The directors of Loftleider then executed as bold a stroke in commercial terms as they had in the exhibition of physical courage which won them their C-47. They calculated that people would be quite happy to fly the Atlantic a little more slowly for a substantially lower fare. They, therefore, began to equip their fleet with second-hand and adapted, but perfectly airworthy, aircraft bought from other airlines. They were right. Despite being forced eventually to equalise fares on European flights and the European legs of transatlantic flights with those of their commercial rivals, they can still offer return fares from Europe to North America which are as much as $152 cheaper than their competitors. Now they can afford, by agreement with the other Nordic countries, to re-equip with new aircraft only (Canadair–Rolls Royce). The success of Loftleider on the basis of its slow flight, low fares policy should give pause for thought to those airlines scrambling for the costly, peace-shattering supersonic planes with which they hope to save a couple of hours flight time. A fortuitous by-product of the presence of us military aircraft has been the successful development of an Icelandic industry.

⊠

But the Icelandic economy owes more to the military presence of foreign troops than just this one by-product. The major consequences of the occupation in 1940 and the build-up of British and then American military bases over the next quarter of a century were twofold: the start of the inflationary spiral, and an added boost in capital and income to the Icelandic economy at a critical period of expansion. Beside these, such social problems as the limitation of the number of Americans allowed into Reykjavík on leave, or the television transmissions from the United States base over which local opinion became so heated in the early 1960s, are relatively unimportant.

In 1939, Iceland was a debtor nation faced with a severe financial crisis owing to shortage of foreign-exchange reserves (the deficit was 12·5 million kronur). At the end of the war, as the result of money brought in by foreign forces as well as the absence of all competing fishing fleets, Iceland was handsomely a creditor nation, with a favourable balance of trade, strong reserves (reaching in 1945 a peak of 581 million kronur),

85

and the resources for a full-scale programme of capital investment. These reserves—together with the vast capital assets created by the occupying forces in the shape of airfields and harbour installations, and the machines and equipment left behind in 1945—launched Iceland into full economic take-off. Moreover, military bases during the war had offered both a substantial outlet for agricultural produce and an opportunity for civilian employment.

Immediately after the war, income from foreign military sources disappeared. Fish catches, particularly herring, fell off, and the foreign ships were back in competition, even though the Icelandic fishing vessels obtained from Sweden after 1944 and from Britain after 1945 were up to date and efficient. A post-war spending spree—although much of it was devoted to necessary capital investment in the fishing industry—landed Iceland in financial difficulties in 1947. Only generous allocations of Marshall Aid sustained investment in the all-important fishing industry and met the balance of payments deficit.

Then, in 1952, came a crucial expansion in activity at the American NATO airbase at Keflavík (founded in 1951) which, by 1953 and 1954, was bringing in foreign-exchange earnings, equivalent to almost 30 per cent of Iceland's commodity exports (27.56 net weighted average). By 1960, this source of revenue had fallen to about $12\frac{1}{2}$ per cent; by 1964, to only 4·6 per cent. The Icelanders have always been very sensitive about their degree of dependence on the military base for foreign-exchange earnings and correspondingly relieved as the part played by these has declined. But it is interesting to note that, from the low point of 1964, the amount brought in by the base had risen by 1966, not only absolutely by $3·5 million, but to 6·9 per cent of total commodity export earnings. With the heavy fall in commodity exports in 1967,[*] the percentage is likely to rise sharply again; and, in present circumstances, the Icelanders are probably glad to be 'embarrassed' once more.

* See page 98 below.

The other major consequence of Iceland's wartime military occupation was in some ways far from beneficial, for the occupation fired a 'revolution of rising expectations' which aroused a rather grasping streak in the Icelander. Since the Allies had not come by invitation, the general philosophy of the increasing number of civilians employed by them was, 'get as much out of them as you possibly can'. This attitude was encouraged by a number of political parties. Although both British and Americans agreed to follow domestic wage levels, the wages they actually paid were substantially higher due to long hours, overtime rates and various upgradings. Take-home pay for someone working for the occupation forces was markedly higher than the Icelanders' own rather depressed standards. The result was an accelerated increase in family incomes and, despite the restrictions on the import of foreign luxury goods caused by the war, almost as rapid a rise in standards of living. Once such expectations had been roused, and satisfied, there could be no going back after the war. There consequently began that inflationary wage-price spiral, which, while it has brought the Icelanders perhaps the second highest individual standard of living in the world, has been the greatest threat to their economic security. (This inflationary pattern is discussed later.) The post-war determination to hold and increase what they had won, even if it meant every Icelander doing two—or at least one and a half—jobs, was strengthened by memories of the pre-war depression years when unemployment was high. Unfortunately the grasping attitude developed, perhaps not unnaturally, towards foreign employers during the war was afterwards to some extent directed towards Icelandic employers, and the present government has only just begun to persuade most of the wage-earning population to recognise the overall effects on the economy of totally unrestrained demands for wage increases.

Perhaps the most staggering aspect of the Icelandic economy is the fact that, despite the limited resources, so much has been accomplished, so high a standard of living achieved. Prices are certainly high, but so are wages. The most distinctive feature of Icelandic incomes is the relatively narrow spread of earnings between the highest and lowest paid.* In 1966, doctors were the top earners with an average of 442,000 kr. a year,† closely followed by trawler skippers, 392,000 kr., while the average income of married workers, skilled and unskilled, and seamen, was 199,550 kr. (1967, 245,500 kr.). Minimum hourly day wages for unskilled workers in 1967 were almost 50 kr. There are very few individuals wealthy by ownership; none of the private trawler or factory owners is such on a great scale. So we find that the very highest paid earn little more than three times the income of the lowest paid. The problem with wages in Iceland is not so much their absolute or relative levels as the rate at which they have increased, on average by 200 per cent between 1960 and 1966 (see Table 19, page 214).

Admittedly, in the scramble in the past two years, the gap between skilled and unskilled workers has been closed even further, but this is not necessarily a good thing in a country in which there is a labour shortage, in spite of the 2 per cent increase of the labour force each year as the country's young population reaches working age (43 per cent of the population were under twenty years of age in 1965). The average Icelander works extremely hard for his money, either by doing between

* Figures given here show gross taxable income, i.e. they include social security transfers, wife and children's earnings plus a low estimate of imputed rent of own housing.

† These figures can be equated with sterling and dollars on the basis of the pre-November 1967 exchange rate of 120 and 43 kr. respectively, but since this rate of exchange was artificially low in terms of real purchasing power, something between this figure and the November 1967 rate of 137 kr. to the pound (a devaluation of 10 per cent) will give roughly accurate equivalents. No attempt has been made here to adjust further to the devaluation of November 1968.

fourteen and sixteen hours overtime on top of his basic forty-four-hour week or by taking a second job. (I met one man, for example, who was both bus driver and school teacher.) The Icelander probably also helps practically in the building of his own house. In 1966, the demand for labour eased fractionally and more noticeably in the summer of 1967 when the traditional, if not always very productive, holiday jobs for the children and students were not always available. The Burfell project was expected to absorb 10 per cent of the labour force in construction in 1967 and 1968 (though, at present, one quarter are specialist workmen from Sweden) so the level of labour demand over-all will probably remain fairly constant. (In fact, in 1968, Burfell engaged barely 2 per cent of all Icelandic labour.) The prospect of unemployment is still a frightening one to Icelanders, and the prime minister's reaction to the prospect of combating inflation through unemployment was as near vehemence as he ever came in his interview with the author. 'Avoiding disturbances in the economy by deliberately permitting unemployment cannot be defended. Inflation is better than unemployment.'

The pattern of wage levels in Iceland has traditionally been set by the fishing industry which experiences great over-all fluctuations both in income levels with variations in catch and also between the different categories (herring and whitefish) of fishermen. Most improvidently, no provision was made against price fluctuations until 1967, and this is not yet comprehensive. High earnings in the herring fleet have not reflected the nation's need to sustain at a high level the whitefish industry and related processing, with its higher rate of export earnings per ton. Government intervention has even been necessary to ward off wholesale transference of investment into the herring industry which even now, as predicted, is experiencing a marked fall in catches. Thus, fishermen have made wage claims based on the highest earning group amongst them. The industrial and service workers, often engaged very much less productively, have based their claims on fishermen's wages; and the farmers, who are guaranteed related income levels by the government price-fixing mechanism, hang their expectations on those of industry. Hence, the very success of the export activities of the fishing industry and the resulting upsurge in wages have set off inflationary demands for imported consumer goods which have largely negated the over-all economic rewards of high foreign-exchange earnings.

The stabilisation of wages has been further complicated by various fluctuations in government policy. In 1960, the statutory link between wages and the cost of living was abolished. Negotiation between employers and unions in the open market, which had been moderated by this provision, was once again given free rein as the sole means of determining wage levels. In 1964, in an attempt to halt inflationary trends, the link was reinstated as part of a general bargain between government and unions. The government thus felt it necessary to try to keep prices down by large consumer subsidies, in particular on food, but was unable to raise additional revenue to pay these since both direct and indirect taxes were included in the cost-of-living index. The new index introduced at the end of 1967 excludes taxes; while this may be a nice piece of economists' double-think, it should enable the government to use direct taxation more effectively as a means of controlling demand. It did seem, however, as if by autumn 1966 an element of sanity had been restored to the situation. The government decided to hold the cost-of-living index at the August level and to introduce a price-freeze, with all increases made subject to government authorisation. As a result, wages remained virtually unchanged until November 1967, by which date the effects of, first, a heavy reduction in government subsidies, and, then, devaluation effected an increase in the cost of living estimated at between 10 and 11 per cent. It remains to be seen, in Iceland as in the United Kingdom, whether the public, certainly more aware in 1967 and 1968 of the implications and requirements of the economic situation than it had been previously, is willing to exercise restraint in wage demands to reap the benefits of devaluation. A coherent wage policy is made even more difficult to attain by the multiplicity of negotiating unions and the lack of any real central union authority.*

❁

In addition to higher wages and consumer subsidies, the Icelander enjoys a very substantial 'invisible' income from educational and welfare services. The tradition of a welfare state in a sense goes back to the period of the first settlers, although in its modern form it is regarded as having been launched in 1936. Under the laws of the first Icelandic Commonwealth, it was a punishable offence to be a victim of poverty caused by one's own crime or negligence. The penalty was loss of all rights of citizenship until the culprit had earned himself an honest living for three years. On the other hand, the inhabitants of each parish were bound by law to help a man restore any loss or destruction of property sustained by fire, or loss of cattle through storm and pestilence. The damage was estimated within a fortnight by a local jury and the assessment met by the man's neighbours. If, without act of God or any fault of his own, a man nevertheless fell into poverty, it was the local magistrate's duty to see that his relatives provided for him. If the relatives were unable to undertake this burden, then the cost of keeping the pauper fed, clothed and housed was met from public funds. This aspect of early welfare lingers still in the legally defined responsibility of parents and children for each other in present-day Iceland.

According to the law, both parents of a legitimate child have an obligation to provide for and 'bring up' the child until it is sixteen. They have also to induce 'good morals' and 'industry' and provide education. After the age of sixteen, the duty to

* See page 124 below.

provide for a child continues 'according to the means' of the parents. Children have a similar obligation to their parents. No distinction is made between legitimate and illegitimate children in regard to parental rights and obligations, except that the paternity of an illegitimate child must be legally established and the father's obligations, other than a contribution to its upbringing, are not enforced.

As with so much welfare legislation in Europe, a great impetus was given by the depression of the 1930s. The key piece of legislation on which the modern Icelandic welfare state is based was a Social Insurance Act in 1936 (substantially revised in 1946), which provided a scheme of sickness and unemployment benefit (the latter, needless to say, scarcely ever called on), old age and disability pensions. To these have since been added the full range of maternity benefits, widows' pensions and compensation to the widows of men accidentally killed during their employment.* This provision is most humanely extended to a woman not married to the victim, but pregnant by him, bringing up his child or who had lived with him for eighteen months. These various benefits were given further coherence by the National Insurance scheme of 1946 which provided, in addition, for comprehensive health services under which the greater part or, in cases of poverty, the whole, of the cost of medical attention, hospital care and medicine, is met by the state. In 1968, Iceland had 267 doctors (which makes a very expensive ratio of one per 750 inhabitants) and forty-five hospitals, most of them very small, except in Rejkjavík, because of the wide and sparsely populated areas they have to serve. Major diseases—such as tubercolosis, once rampant—have been well nigh stamped out, and infant mortality, approximately one in 1,000 is amongst the lowest in the world. The isolated areas are linked to the medical network by an almost

* Some other important welfare legislation dates: 1928, Factory Inspection; 1935, Employment Exchanges; 1942, Eight-Hour Day; 1943, Two-Weeks' Paid Holiday; 1952, Safety Legislation.

all-weather air ambulance service and by a system of district midwives and nurses.

An unusual feature of the Icelandic social security system is its unified structure; from the outset, it has been administered by a single ministry, the State Insurance Board. A uniform system of financing was introduced in 1946, by which a flat-rate contribution is levied on all employed persons, independent of income but regulated by price zones—rural or urban—sex and marital status only. The exception to this method of finance is that whereby compensation is paid for employment injuries; this fund is completely subscribed by the employers. The cost of social insurance is met, approximately, 50 per cent from public funds, 40 per cent from the insured and 10 per cent from the employers. Many insured people also receive both tax allowances and direct cash benefits for their dependent children under sixteen, for whom, however, they are inescapably responsible financially until that age. The Icelandic insurance system differed until recently from most of those prevailing in Europe by virtue of the fact that some benefits were dependent on a means test, now abolished; also that in certain circumstances those in receipt of poor relief (the closest British equivalent of which is National Assistance) might later be required to repay the sum received to the parish if they were reasonably able to do so. In total, about one-tenth of the national income is spent on social services (see Table 18, page 213).

The single-class structure of Iceland, together with the long traditions of independence and self-sufficiency have naturally coloured the growth of the social-security system and the Icelandic attitude to the welfare state. The emphasis on the care for the dependants of the man killed at work, for example, is only natural in a community where so many earn their living by hazarding their lives to chance of the ungentle sea. Welfare in Iceland has not grown from the charitable patronage of the rich but has always been a collective activity. There is, therefore, neither shame nor greed associated with the taking of

93

benefits, and the comprehensive safety-net supplied by the social services does not in any way seem to have diminished the mutual sense of responsibility for each other's welfare among families or communities.

The other great free amenity, or rather necessity, for Icelanders, is education. This is compulsory for all between the ages of seven and fifteen, and schooling is given with two very short breaks only, during the eight dark months of the autumn, in winter and early spring. The curriculum, though somewhat heavily biased to the humanities and verbal arts, is wide-ranging and imaginative. Every Icelandic child, for example, is taught to swim—in a well-heated pool—before he or she leaves primary school. Many of the schools, particularly those serving the rural areas, are boarding schools, and families are given a limited degree of choice in their children's attendance at these if no local day-school is available.

However, no one pretends that universal comprehensive formal education is as all-embracing in practice as in theory. In rural areas, with various exceptions which are permitted and several which are not, a child may well receive much less than the full quota of basic schooling; but it must be made clear that these cases are very much the exception.* The essential point in Iceland is that a child is brought up in an educated society and learns far more than is usual in other countries from his family and community environment. You may, indeed, meet quite a few Icelanders whose formal education has been brief, perhaps totalling not more than three to four years all told; but it is rare, very rare, to meet an ill-educated Icelander.

* Rural school districts may exempt children from attendance until they are eight, nine, or even ten; and in areas where the children are served by boarding schools, they are divided into three batches, each having thirteen weeks at school in the year. If 'touring' school, for which the teacher visits a small group of children living in different farmhouses by turns in the most isolated districts, is still necessary, two months' instruction is given. It would thus be possible (but unlikely) for a child to receive a total of only ten to fourteen months of compulsory basic schooling.

After the basic schooling is over, optional secondary schooling, with a different bias towards academic or technical subjects as appropriate to the student, is available on payment of a nominal fee, as is access to the University of Rejkjavík, which has just over 1,500 students in five major faculties: medicine and dentistry, law and commerce, theology, philosophy (including the humanities), and engineering. About 1,000 Icelanders go abroad for their university or higher education; most go to Europe, in particular Denmark, and some to America. It can thus be seen that the Icelander's high standard of living is further enhanced by the free or low-cost benefits he derives from various community services.

❧

On the debit side, the principal item has been the headlong rate of inflation. Over the years, this has amounted to more than 10 per cent per annum. The annual increase in the cost-of-living index (in percentage increase over the preceding year, consisting of goods and services, food, heating, electricity, etc., clothing, footwear, etc., miscellaneous, rent and direct taxes, and social security contributions) was 10·9 in 1962; in 1963, 12·9; in 1964, 19·3; in 1965, 7·3; in 1966, 10·7; in 1967, 5·6. Between 1960 and 1965, the cost of living increased by 75 per cent. In the same period, the prices of both consumer goods and construction went up 90 per cent—in the case of construction partly because the yearly increase in demand has usually been over 10 per cent.

Prices outside Rejkjavík tend to be higher; for example, in Isafjord a pot of coffee for two with four pieces of plain cake in a seamen's hostel cost 100 kronur as against between 60 and 75 kronur in Rejkjavík. (All prices here are at the pre-November 1967 exchange-rate of 120 kronur to the pound). The only times at which the cost-of-living index has remained stable (and then only briefly) have been during the wage-freezes and when a wages/cost-of-living link operated—as, for example, during the

95

price-freeze, and partially successful wage-freeze, from October 1966 to October 1967. Otherwise, the inflationary process launched on the economy by the 1939–45 war has continued unabated. There have been minor modifications of policy, but today, in Bjarni Benediktsson's own words: 'We rely on the same measures we have used before.'

These measures have proved inadequate in the past and there is little reason to suppose that they will be any more effective in the future, except, perhaps, that the people are at least now more alert to the consequences of uncontrolled inflation. The Icelander bears a very heavy load in indirect taxation which is reflected in the rise of the consumer-goods price index; but he does not fare too badly on direct taxation. The standard rates of national income tax are only three: 9, 18, and 27 per cent respectively. Municipal taxes vary but are usually of the order of 10, 20, and 30 per cent. Both state and municipal income taxes are levied on net basis after deduction of some personal items, allowances,* interest, *per capita* taxes and net

	Income net of personal deductions (kr.)	Income before personal deductions (kr.)
State income tax, rate %		
9	0–47,800	186,100–233,900
10	47,800–80,000	233,900–266,100
27	80,000–up	266,100–up
Muncipal income tax, rate %		
10	0–25,800	90,300–116,100
20	25,800–77,400	116,100–167,700
30	77,400–up	167,700–up
There are additional taxes on property (etc.)		

* The current rates for personal allowances (in kronur) are: *state income tax*—single person 103,200, couple 144,500, child (under sixteen) 20,700; *municipal income tax*—single person 45,200, couple 64,500, child (under sixteen) 12,900.

property taxes, and also the municipal tax after deduction of the same tax of the previous year, if promptly paid. In order to give meaning to these rates, it is best to assume a family of a certain size, let us say a couple and two children. There are additional taxes on property and on corporation profits; social-security contributions are deducted from pay; and motor vehicles are taxed separately.

With this scale of taxation, the Icelanders have enjoyed a very real increase in their standard of living since the war both in cash-income terms and in amenities. The average Icelander (and again we must remember that the range of variation from the mean is very small) is housed with far greater comfort and spaciousness, not to mention greater elegance and taste, than the average European or even American. Certainly, squalid and vulgar houses are to be found in Reykjavík but they are conspicuous by their rarity. The Icelander is as well-fed, clothed and transported, and as well looked after by welfare and educational services, as any citizen in the world. The women in particular are, almost without exception, well-dressed and visit the hairdressers regularly as a matter of course.

The 1960s saw a very rapid expansion of the Icelandic economy, with GNP increasing at an average rate of 5·1 per cent from 1961 to 1968. Trading terms also improved and thus national income went up even more rapidly (see Table 15, page 211). The level of demand also remained high, although one encouraging factor was the amount of investment (see Table 16, page 211) particularly considered in the light of the disincentive to accumulate reserves of working capital when such a rapid rate of inflation prevailed. The balance of payments position remained good and for most of the period foreign-exchange reserves increased substantially (see Table 14, page 210).

It seems a very healthy comparative picture but it is not securely based, although Iceland's general economic strength is far greater than before the war. The fluctuating cycles of the

Icelandic economy have been exaggerated in the past two decades by the coincidence of poor catches with poor export prices and good catches with high export prices. Iceland's inflationary spiral and its foreign-exchange difficulties are reflected in the fortunes of the krona over the years, which in terms of US dollars is worth scarcely a tenth of what it was twenty years ago (see Table 20, page 214).

By 1966, it looked as though Iceland was entering another lean period. The expansion began to slow down in that year, and 1967 witnessed a sharp reversal of its economic fortunes: export prices fell heavily (by 30 per cent) and so did catches, resulting in a drop of 1·5 per cent in GNP in volume for 1967 and an even greater fall, 8 per cent, in national income. The current account on the balance of payments ran up a deficit which may be over $50 million (equivalent to 9 per cent of GNP) despite capital imports and special investments. Foreign exchange reserves fell sharply and by the end of 1967 were down to $18 million, or the unhealthily narrow margin of the cost of eight to ten weeks' commodity imports.

In 1968, the fall in prices for exports, especially whitefish products, appeared at first to have been halted, but by the end of the year a fall of a further 15 per cent seemed inevitable. In November 1967, the government, which, as is the wont of governments, had been categorically denying any thought of the devaluation which leading businessmen were urging as essential,* was presented with a golden opportunity when sterling was devalued and it was able to follow suit without loss of face. It not only devalued by 24·6 per cent (10 per cent more than the United Kingdom), but introduced a number of other measures at the same time. Consumer subsidies were reduced to the level of August 1966; property tax was increased, and so was the tax on tobacco and alcohol; social-security premiums and hospital fees went up, and a reduction in government

---

* A number expressed this view vehemently, if not for attributable quotation, in interviews with the author in summer 1967.

expenditure was planned. (It was envisaged that the budgetary saving would probably be used to cut tariffs and increase social-security benefits.) Exports should have benefited markedly and the balance-of-payments position have been restored to health. But continued pressure for higher wages and the failure of the 1967 devaluation to reverse the fall in the value of exports showed that futher remedies were needed. In desperation, the government increased and repeated the dose of its previous medicine, devaluing in November 1968 by an additional swingeing 35·2 per cent. The efficacy of this latest step has yet to be judged.

Inflation is having a disastrous effect on the competitive strength of the all-important nascent industries providing diversification. For example, a factory in Akureyrí manufacturing woollen goods, and in particular the popular Icelandic sweaters, has in the past five years had wage increases of 105 per cent in response to worker demands. Production techniques have improved but over-all costs have still risen by 100 per cent, while the price of the goods in the European market has had to remain unchanged. In other words there is as yet no evidence that Iceland has really escaped from its perennial economic difficulties. Can it, in fact, ever do so?

The OECD report on the Icelandic economy for 1968 urged that the country seize the opportunity to concentrate manufacturing into larger units—presumably in a large population centre. Two leading Icelandic economists, Jonas Haralz and Arni Vilhjalmsson, gave their analysis and implicit solution to the problem in a paper published as long ago as 1960.

Out of the struggle for independence and intense nationalism of the early century has grown a society which is not only nationalistic, but also highly democratic and egalitarian, and which in its fear of authority has placed the core of power in Parliament and stripped the executive power of several essential functions. In Parliament again, the centre

99

of gravity has remained in the outlying rural and semi-rural areas and has only to a limited extent been transferred to the new urban centres. This type of society may still, like nationalism did in the early century, provide a powerful initiative for economic action, albeit not always an action judiciously chosen. As time has gone by, however, its effects in the other direction, that of hampering economic growth, have become more and more important. The dilution of executive power makes it difficult to formulate and carry out coherent economic policies. Here lies another basic reason for inflation and the balance-of-payments deficits. The prevailing egalitarianism has also, through its shaping of tax policy and wage structure, stifled capital accumulation and reduced economic incentives. Lastly, nationalism has been effective in preventing the participation of foreign capital in the country's economic development.[3]

The concentration of industry and the strengthening of executive authority to secure the implementation of carefully calculated economic controls might certainly provide a solution to Iceland's economic ills, but it can only do so at a price which Icelanders have to assess to see if it is worth paying.

The paper just quoted rightly states: 'These three factors, the high level of education, nationalism and the characterisation of natural resources, have continued to influence the economic development of the country, promoting it in some ways, hampering it in others and shaping it in a way all of its own.' Nature's limitations can be tackled under most systems. But what of nationalism? What of the dilution of executive power? What of the 'prevailing egalitarianism'? If these 'defects' are to be overcome as a conscious and deliberate act of economic policy, then the corollary of giving absolute priority to the establishment of an efficient and flourishing economy must be an authoritarian executive. This might well lead to the negation of Iceland's democratic tradition, the destruction of the spirit of nationalism which sets its people apart as a distinctive entity, the concentration of a still higher proportion of the population in Reykjavík to the detriment of the rest of the country, and the creation of a class-conscious plutocracy in place of the easy and creative intercourse of Iceland's one-class society.*

It is not for an outsider to advise on such a choice, which is not an easy one for those involved; but I suspect that, as in the past Icelanders have endured rather than been moulded by their economic circumstances, so in the future they will avoid the mistake of treating their unique society as nothing but the sum of its constituent economic units.

* Cf. Constitution, Art. 78 (page 196 below).

5

State and Social Institutions

ECONOMIC CIRCUMSTANCES, while responsible for the recent upsurge of materialism which may in due course have much influence on the Icelandic character, cannot be said to have moulded it; prosperity is of too recent origin. We have seen how the Althing in the Commonwealth period, while more than just a social gathering or a court of justice or a democratic hustings, was not the prime mover in Icelandic society; and, indeed, from the thirteenth to the mid-nineteenth century was little more than a cypher. The Church, Roman and Reformed, which succeeded the Althing as the major institutional force in Iceland also lost its influence in time. An examination of those more modern estates of the realm, the press and the trade unions, will show the same strange immunity of the Icelandic people to formal influences. The machinery of Icelandic politics is all-instructive in this respect.

Party politics is a relatively recent development in Iceland. During the nineteenth century, all efforts by a uniformly impoverished and frustrated people were concentrated on the struggle for independence. Only at the turn of the century, when it was already clear that some form of independence was inevitable, did any political divisions appear, and these only concerned the form which independence might take. There were those who favoured acceptance of the definition of Iceland's role within the Danish realm set out by a joint commission of Danes and Icelanders reporting in 1908. This 'Home Rule' party was, however, defeated by the Independence party which, making far more extensive demands, succeeded in getting the 1908 proposals rejected. In 1916, two more parties entered the lists: an Agrarian party, forerunner of the present Progressives and supported in general by the rural co-operative movement; and a Labour party formed on the lines of the Scandinavian social-democrat parties and drawing its support in the main from the urban labouring population. The two original groups, the Home Rulers and the Independence party, evolved during the 1920s into conservative and liberal parties respectively. But, in 1929, they resolved their differences and merged to form a renewed Independence party.

This party now leads the government, and from its antecedents describes itself as liberal-conservative in policy. Its attitudes have grown naturally from its insistence, during the struggle to break free of Danish rule, on complete financial independence as an essential first step. It is thus today the most forthright champion of free trade and private enterprise.

The 1930s were a period of similar divisions and regroupings of parties on the left which derived their inspiration from the gradual organisation of Icelandic labour and from the social-democrat parties of Scandinavia. In 1930, some members of the Labour movement broke away to form the Icelandic Communist party and affiliated to the Third International. Eight years later, the majority of the Communists, disillusioned with both their own lack of political success and by the debasement of Marxist ideals in Stalin's Russia, reunited with a large part of the Labour party, which had remained in being, to form the People's Alliance, or Socialist party. In all this, left-wing politics in Iceland conformed to the 'front populaire' trend in Europe.

Although there have since been in all parties attempts by various splinter-groups to launch new movements, none of them has come to anything, and the party battle-lines today are drawn up, on paper at least, much as they were in 1938. Representation in the Althing has shown only small variations.

State of the Parties in the Althing, 1946–67

	1946	1949	1953	1956	1959 Spring	1959 Autumn	1963	1967
Independence Party	20	19	21	19	20	24	24	23
Progressive Party	13	17	16	17	19	17	19	18
Labour Party	9	7	6	8	6	9	8	9
People's Alliance	10	9	7	8	7	10	9	9+1
Other	—	—	2	—	—	—	—	—
Totals	52	52	52	52	52	60	60	60

The outcome of this nice balance of forces in Icelandic politics has been the prevalence of government by coalition. For only twelve years in the last half-century has a single party been in power, and during the past twenty-five years there has been no one-party government in Iceland. (The present administration is a coalition of the Independence party and the Labour party.) Even more astonishing, perhaps, is the fact that every single party has been in a coalition government at some time with every other party.

Such a pattern seems likely to persist in view of the electoral reforms introduced before the 1967 election. Hitherto, the country had been divided into constituencies, each of which returned one or two members to the Althing. This direct election was accompanied by the distribution of a number of seats among the parties in such a way as to ensure that each party's total representation in the Althing reflected as far as possible its share of the total national vote. These additional members were chosen in descending order from the respective parties' national list of candidates, and alternative members were also chosen for these seats who substitute for them in the event of the first member's inability to attend the Althing. But in 1967, a new system was introduced which replaced the single- or double-member constituencies by eight much larger constituencies. These return five or six members in the various provinces, and twelve in Reykjavík. The election thus becomes almost totally proportional in nature for, as well as the regional party lists in the eight constituencies, the old system of balancing the representation from national lists is retained.

Under such an electoral system, the means by which party candidates are chosen and the degree of involvement of the local population in that choice becomes, in many ways, the real test of the degree of democracy to be found in the political system as a whole. In Iceland the parties work on very similar lines. In each regional constituency, the party members elect from among their number a council whose function is to discuss policy, present resolutions to annual national congresses and raise funds. At election time it is this council which puts up the candidates' list for the region, in the order in which candidates will be returned depending on the party's share in the regional vote. The parties may also put up national lists. Thus, the would-be MP has to be careful not to offend too many sectional interests. In most countries where the list system is operated, the result is generally a drab succession of party hacks trooping into parliament. In Iceland, the power of party patronage is diminished by the individualism of nearly all the people on any list, in whatever order they may be placed, and by the readiness of an Icelander to form a splinter-group (as in Reykjavík) at the drop of a contradictory opinion. These, however, remain only moderating factors, and the trend is towards party men. Probably because of the development of consensus selection, the Althing is depressingly lacking both in young and female members. (In the present parliament, as in its predecessor, there is only one woman member, and only four members are under the age of forty.)

The rarity of women in parliament at first seems astonishing in a country where there is no more class division by sex than there is by wealth, and where, from the very earliest times, women have been accorded not only equality before the law but very real partnership. Icelandic women have always had the right both to divorce and also to property protection in divorce. The Sagas recount several instances of this custom, and reveal even more telling cases in which the woman is clearly an equal, even the dominating influence, not by the exercise of feminine wiles but from male respect for her intelligence or strength of character. But Icelandic women also have, both in life and more recent literature, a domestic reputation for being somewhat frivolous. It is hard for an outsider to tell whether or not it is justified. Is what appears mere frivolity rather an extrovert capacity for enjoying life which happens to contrast with the manifestly greater reticence of the Icelandic male? Certainly, the revolution in consumer habits was most eagerly seized on—as it would have been in any country with so long a history of poverty—by the women. But is this all there is to it? I met very few women in key positions in any walk of life, none in business, none in the civil service, none in the professions. I did meet extremely capable women journalists, artists and many wives of parsons, farmers, business men and others who far outshone in intelligent conversation any equally random selection from similar European, let alone American, social and occupational strata. Their contributions to discussions in politics, the arts, economics, fishing techniques, were treated neither patronisingly nor humorously nor contemptuously, but just as contributions to be judged on the merit of their content and expression. I thus gained a striking impression of a natural acceptance of an intellectual and personal equality which made quite superfluous any emphasis on the occupational equality with which English women, among others, are so obsessed. It is only an outsider's theory, but it is reasonable to suspect that, in a society in which opportunity is really equal, women do not participate in a great many supposedly prestige-bestowing activities (including politics) from choice.

When the party list of candidates has been drawn up, the election campaign is conducted much as in all parliamentary democracies in Western Europe, but there are a number of different emphases. The highlights of the Icelandic contest are provided by the public confrontation of candidates. At meetings which often go on until the small hours, and at which time is fairly divided, they take turn and turn about to argue their case before the electors. What a contrast to a British election, where the candidates generally avoid such public debate lest their mediocrity be exposed! Television is not a feature of Icelandic elections yet, although, with the spread of stations outside Reykjavík, it is bound to become so in the 1970s. Debates are conducted on the totally impartial radio service, which ensures approximately equal time to all parties. Election expenditure is unlimited, so it is hard to gauge what is actually spent, but it seems to exceed the investment made by most European political parties. Funds are raised by personal subscription and donations, but the main source of them is the running of regular national lotteries by each of the parties.

Campaign posters are rare, but direct-mail literature is increasingly used. Highly efficient polling-day organisations are, as elsewhere, often the key to success in getting an additional member of your party list elected, particularly in the rural areas with their small electorates. Partly as the result of the efficiency of local party organisation, but more because of the Icelander's consciousness of civic duty and his pleasure in participating in national events, the poll is nearly always at least 85 per cent and not uncommonly in the high 90s. The same pattern is reflected in municipal and local elections, but with personal influence playing a more important role than party allegiance.

Once elected, in what kind of parliament and constitutional system does the new MP find himself? His membership of parliament is, certainly, not one that will of itself provide him with a decent living wage, so he must either retain a business or profession, or (as is the case with about half of the members of the Althing) make a living as a professional politician: part MP, part political journalist or party or union functionary. He may be spared this double existence if he is fortunate enough to get a seat in the cabinet, in which case he will receive a monthly salary ranging from 33,101 kronur to the prime minister's 33,961.

When the elected member arrives in the Althing, after the process of swearing in, he will find the first vote is another election by which the total membership of sixty is divided into an upper chamber (*Efri Deild*) of twenty members and a lower chamber (*Nethri Deild*) of forty, either of which may initiate legislation. It can thus be seen that a government, or rather coalition, needs an over-all majority of two to control parliament. The sixty members meet jointly for certain matters as a single chamber: for example, at certain stages in the debate and vote on the budget and on constitutional matters. If constitutional amendments or changes in the status or the organisation of the Church are made, the Althing is immediately dissolved and an election held. Only if the newly elected

Althing endorses the change does it become law (as in 1959, when the number of members was increased from fifty-two to sixty). There may sit among the members of the Althing also one or two cabinet ministers who are not elected members of parliament but have been appointed by the president at the prime minister's request and have the right to speak (when called by the president of each house, who is elected by the members of the Althing chambers) and move resolutions, but not to vote. The executive grows out of, and is firmly controlled by, the elected Althing.

The constitution is protected from abuse by both legislature and executive by the role of the president of the republic. Elected every four years by universal suffrage, the president's assent is needed to all legislation (although, in the normal course of events, it can no more be refused than the British monarch's), and he may intervene in constitutional matters. He also fixes the number of ministers, appoints them and receives their resignations, after consulting the prime minister, whom he also appoints. He has the right to call and dissolve parliament. He may also issue provisional laws during a recess of the Althing, which must be ratified as soon as it reassembles, or lapse. The president can veto legislation, which then becomes subject to a referendum in which, if approved, it becomes law despite the president's veto.

The importance of the presidency in maintaining a balance in Icelandic politics is clear. Although, in some respects, the post is regarded as non-political, there are occasions when the presidential election is packed with political significance. The most recent, held in July 1968, is a good example. Dr Gunnar Thorodsen, Iceland's ambassador to Denmark, might almost have been termed the official candidate, having as he did the backing of the ruling parties. He was, however, defeated by Professor Kristjan Eldjarn, a fifty-one-year-old archaeologist and director of the National Museum, who obtained 64·9 per cent of the vote. Particularly galling for the government was its man's overwhelming defeat in the north and west where, despite what the government has not unjustifiably felt to be a generous policy of regional development, the local electors gave its man scarcely a single vote. Many Icelanders, in fact, interpret this election not just as the voters' preference for one man over another but as a vote of no confidence in the present government, attributable to the country's present perilous economic situation.

The private member's most effective weapon, as in Britain, remains the parliamentary question. In Iceland, these are nearly always given in writing two or three weeks before they are to be answered, but the president of either chamber may allow supplementary debate. The first parliamentary function in which the new member will participate is the budget debate which begins the annual session, usually in October. The vote at the end of each of three readings of the budget, or any other bill not dealing with constitutional matters in the separate chambers or the united Althing, is decided by a straight majority, but half the members are necessary to form a quorum. The proceedings of these debates and other parliamentary business are open to the public, except when the Althing votes to sit in camera, and are published in a regular parliamentary gazette. The new member of the Althing may also introduce a bill as a private member. This, despite difficult working conditions and time-shortage, is treated like any other government bill, for Iceland's parliament is still able to get through all the business it wishes to handle.

Icelandic parliamentarians span a wide range of attitudes and influences. Of the several I met in addition to the prime minister, two stand out in contrast as giving something of the total flavour of Icelandic politics; Einar Olgeirsson, once a communist MP, and Sigurdur Bjarnasson, a prominent MP in the Independence party.

Einar lives modestly in a small first-floor flat in one of the less plushy parts of Reykjavík. A slight, grey-haired man of quiet voice, and at first seemingly of a quiet nature, greets you undemonstratively at the ground-floor door. A teacher, or university don, you think. The first thing you see on the landing outside his door is a small table on which lie a few books. These, you realise a moment later, are only the over-spill, the migrant element from the huge stiff-bound population of volumes running to thousands which, in lovingly ordered ranks, occupy every inch of wall-space in the living rooms. The furniture is sparse, simple, even cheap, while a wealth, in both senses, of books encloses it. Books mark the starting point of our conversation, for Einar has not only a most comprehensive political library, particularly on Marxist and socialist philosophy, but a number of fine literary works and some rare editions. He enthuses about one in particular, the works of William Morris, in which he draws attention to certain passages and takes pride that Morris came to socialism through Iceland and its Sagas.

We turn to politics, and with precision and brilliance he analyses the developments of the society in which he lives and its present problems. He sees Iceland as two nations, the young and the old. The old subject to spiritual influences, in the broadest sense, and in living communion with the Saga characters; the young subject only to economic influences. He pinpoints the formative effects of the length of the tribal period of society in Iceland, the transitional brevity of feudalism, the absence of the concept of a state, as opposed to a nation, and the neglect, therefore, of the possibilities of the state. Historically, the Icelandic state, in so far as there was one, was a foreign state and therefore inimical to the average Icelander; and this antipathy continues to the present day. This pattern produced individuality and fostered the value of man against the value of money. Now it is all changing. . . . Then suddenly, after so much thoughtful exposition, the bugaboo of 'capitalism' is produced to carry the blame for all Iceland's ills. But Einar is too intellectually honest to leave mere assertion unqualified

for long. Capitalism, he allows, has undoubtedly saved the
country from mass emigration.

It is hard to get him to talk about himself. He would rather
recount the fortunes of the party: its foundation in 1930 and
membership of only 700 or so; its first three members of parliament, of whom he was one, in 1937; the collapse of the party
as a separate entity in 1938 and the emergence of the People's
Alliance, implying no hope of its revival but at least a place
of refuge for some of its objectives. Then he recalls the party's
opposition to the Allied occupation during the last war and the
vigorous denunciations of it in the party paper which resulted
in his deportation to Britain along with half-a-dozen colleagues
both from the paper and from the u-boat-vulnerable western
fjords. He laughs about it without resentment. He ascribes to
the People's Alliance the important achievement of persuading
the post-war coalition, in which he was a partner, to invest the
capital accumulation of the war-engendered prosperity in the
fishing fleet which is the basis of Iceland's economic expansion.
But the Alliance is not a 'people's party' in the communist
sense; its basis is Marxist socialism rather than Leninism; and,
although Einar is no longer active in politics (albeit still wield-
ing some influence) the compromise seems to suit him, enabling
him to reconcile his regret, nostalgia almost, for the society of
poor, historical Iceland with his desire to see modern, wealthy
Iceland a socialist state.

According to Sigurdur Bjarnasson, socialism is, in practical
terms, a dead duck. It is one of those sets of dogmas, like the
Oder–Neisse line in Germany or racial equality in Britain or
America which, by historically conditioned reflex, springs to
the lips of some politicians but which would frighten them out
of their wits if they had to execute them. He is blunt about the
coalition partnership of his party, the largest in the Althing,
with the social-democrats of the Labour party. These, he asserts,
feel obliged to profess such socialist tenets as state ownership
and control of industry, but in practice are not prepared to push

these policies to the point where it would cost them their place in the coalition and the opportunity directly to exercise power and influence on the conduct of government affairs. He speaks with the voice of a political journalist—which, as political editor of *Morgunblathith,* is exactly what he is—but also tempers his remarks with the reservations of the careful politician, perhaps even regretting his frankness a little and qualifying it.

Sigurdur's manner and style is the antithesis of Einar's. This is the man of affairs at the centre of action. I met him, beyond receptionists and ante-rooms, in a luxuriously furnished large office with a fine outlook on the centre of Reykjavík. His greeting was affable, confident, experienced, and he fenced with the interviewer's questions with a dexterity of parry which belied his large frame. Where the ground was clear, he was blunt and decisive; where obscured, oblique. One felt that his diagnosis of Iceland's ills, so different from Einar's, was being made by someone who analysed in the light of being subsequently called on to act, to whom the problems were of manageable proportions. Swiftly he dismissed the opposition parties. The Progressives: claiming to be radical, but in practice only opportunist with an ill-defined policy and the backing of the highly political co-operatives. The People's Alliance: communist-dominated by five to three. The smaller parties: damned to an ineffectual bleat. The problem with Iceland today is that the young do not know the hard fight for existence which has formed the character and attitude of Icelanders over thirty-five. They want everything at once and cannot be made to realise the country's basic economic problems. They take everything for granted and think only of amusement, with a consequent weakening of their self-reliance. They are physically fit and often even brilliant, but too irresponsible. Sigurdur himself has been an MP for twenty-five years. Parliamentarian, company director, lawyer and editor, his is the philosophy of *real politik.* When people decry the professional politician and belittle his role and status, Sigurdur simply draws attention to the large numbers of people who try to become parliamentarians every election time.

These, of course, are two diametrically opposed analyses and attitudes, recognising in common only the divisions between age and youth—which is at least partly attributable to the inescapable classification of both men in the first group—and the influence of radically changed economic circumstances on political and social attitudes. The Progressives would hotly deny the accusation of opportunism. Certainly, there have been contradictory statements, on foreign policy in particular, from different groups within the Progressive party; but, in fact, it presents on the whole a coherent picture, speaking up for the all-important agrarian and rural interests, motivated by the philosophy of the co-operative movement and representing a responsible and reasonable alternative to the present government.

It is not only the Independence and the Labour parties which are reconciling their differences. Expediency may play its part in that rapprochement, but the evolution of consensus politics in Iceland, as in the rest of Europe, is a far more important factor. At the same time, we should be aware that, if conservatives and social democrats are co-operating to the extent that it is hard to differentiate between them, in Iceland as elsewhere, this is mainly because the outstanding differences between them are now matters of history rather than contemporary issues. They are unlikely to amalgamate in the foreseeable future, for the leading men in both groups set too much store by the prestige they feel is bestowed by their positions within the separate party organisations. But there seems no reason why, in government at least, they could not co-operate indefinitely. As is usual in coalitions, the junior partners are benefiting electorally at the expense of the senior, but the changes are only marginal.

The actual shifts of power and politics are relatively unimportant in following our theme of the influence of institutional life on the Icelandic character. The system has been clearly designed to prevent a concentration of power, the parties are subject to the influence of strong individualists, and parliament itself remains the centre of authority. The Icelanders are never in doubt that they will use their political institutions rather than succumb to them.

❊

The same is true of the legal institutions which cater for the security of a generally law-abiding people and the contentious needs of citizens who have become far less litigious than their forebears. The laws enacted by the Althing are unobtrusively enforced by a legal machinery which rests lightly on the people.

The main burden of both enforcing and interpreting the law rests on the local magistrates in the sixteen districts and eight towns. These magistrates are all professional lawyers (there is no difference between barristers and solicitors in Iceland) and have largely inherited the dual legal and executive functions of the old *gothard* system. That is to say, as well as presiding over the courts of first instance, they are also the local chiefs of police (except in Reykjavík where this is a separate office) and the officials principally responsible for the collection of taxes and rates in their districts. The prisoner who finds himself before a district court will not be tried by jury, but he will be assumed innocent until he is proved guilty. He also has the right to be defended by a professional lawyer (if he does not wish to defend himself as some do with spectacular success), the fees being met by the state if he cannot afford them. The duty of trying to prove the prisoner's guilt rests with the Office of the Public Prosecutor. This, like the drafting of legislation, used to be a function of the Ministry of Justice, but it has now been delegated to a separate department. Should the prisoner be found guilty, he has an automatic right of appeal to a court of second instance, which is the Supreme Court in Reykjavík, consisting of five judges. This body also exercises jurisdiction in interpreting and enforcing the constitution. It will be appreciated that a two-tier system is all that a country as small as Iceland can afford to sustain.

The lower courts' sentences cannot exceed a maximum of five years; longer sentences must be passed by the Supreme Court. The maximum penalty exacted by the Icelandic law is, technically, life imprisonment for the most serious offences against the state or the life of the president, for murder, the more serious bodily assaults, attacks on women, and the abduction of children. However, no 'life sentence' in the literal sense has been passed for fifty years, though there are currently six long-term prisoners to whom the expression may be applied. If a convicted man's appeal is unsuccessful, his last hope lies in a presidential pardon. It may be that his offence does not merit imprisonment as punishment, but the Icelandic system lacks any equivalent of the British probation service and the only alternatives open to the court are to pass a suspended sentence or to order the prisoner into institutional care if he is clearly suffering from mental illness. If he is sent to prison, in the new state prison, he can earn up to one-third remission of sentence by good behaviour.

Civil actions (and this applies also to labour disputes) may be first subject to a conciliation attempt by a local appointed lay board with certain limited powers to make awards in matters of minor debt. These have not been much used in the past forty years. There are also special courts to deal with some maritime and commercial cases. In addition, Iceland has a High Court consisting of fifteen members drawn from the legal profession and the various local councils. This court deals with matters concerning the conduct of ministers of the government which do not properly fall under the constitutional jurisdiction of the Supreme Court.

The most notable feature of the Icelandic legal system to a British observer is the total absence of trial by jury in criminal cases. While this may be regarded as a fundamental liberty in a country like Britain, it is much more difficult of implementation in one like Iceland. Until recent times—and even now only in urban areas—the gathering together of sufficiently large numbers of jurors to obtain the benefits of trial by jury would have been a difficult, costly and socially disruptive process. Trials are held in open court, and the local magistrate has always had something of a representative character. An even more effective safeguard against any abuse or denial of justice is that the nation has always been, and still is, sufficiently small, intelligent and articulate for the public to act as a kind of jury in reserve, ready to protest at any miscarriage of justice in the courts.

Complete independence of the judiciary cannot be said to exist at the lower levels. The constitution protects judges from being removed from office by the government, but this protection applies only to those without administrative posts; the modern '*gothi*' are thus excluded. However, in the Supreme Court, where the constitution is interpreted and judgement passed on ministerial actions, the independence of the judiciary is indisputable. Judges without administrative posts can only be removed after due procedure in the courts.

One of the main problems of law maintenance in Iceland is the difficulty of recruiting policemen when wages in other occupations are so much more attractive. The proportion of policemen to citizens in Reykjavík is two per thousand, in the rural areas slightly lower. But, in fact, the police are not faced with any major growth in crime as far as the statistics (admittedly rather inadequate) can show. The principal offences are drunkenness (for which the raw materials are provided by the government monopoly liquor stores—Iceland has no 'pubs'), brawling and petty theft. There are very few crimes of violence and very few signs of their increasing.* While a first offence

* There were two shooting murders in 1968 to add to the one in 1967, referred to in chapter 7. These in percentage terms give a rise of 100 per cent in two successive years, but this is scarcely significant.

117

for drunkenness might receive a fine of 3,000 kronur (£25), drunken driving always earns a ten-day prison sentence for a first offence, with a maximum penalty of one year.

The legal system meets all the modest demands made on it by social conditions in Iceland, but it certainly has very little effect in shaping them. Rather, it indicates the advanced state of civilisation enjoyed in Iceland when measured in terms of the easy relationship of the citizen to society and to his fellow citizens under the law.

❃

Equally marginal has become the influence of the Icelandic Church. The established Lutheran Church was once the hub of Icelandic life, both spiritual and social, but roads and aircraft and Reykjavík have largely destroyed its standing and much of its influence. In the closed and isolated communities of Iceland before the First World War, the churches were the focal points for local life, the places at which the scattered farmers met, their business was discussed, their entertainments planned, their off-spring paraded in the matrimonial ring. But today they are only empty shells. It is true that you cannot go far in Iceland without coming across one of these old churches, usually still in good repair, its corrugated iron roof and tiny spire painted the usual green or red, its corrugated iron walls clean white. Inside, too, it is often neat, with trim pews and even, surprisingly for those whose Lutheran contacts have been with the more austere German form, brightly decorated altars and pulpits. But at the Sunday service most of the country churches are ill-attended and it has become harder to get organists than parsons. Even the architecturally exciting churches of Reykjavík, although relatively more full, cannot claim all their congregation as devout worshippers. Other denominations, though legally tolerated, present little competition and the state of religion in Iceland stands or falls by the established Lutheran Church.

Just as the parish church is no longer the centre of social intercourse, so the parson is no longer the fount of wisdom and learning for his district. But, in the country districts at least, this
change is not so far-reaching. The parish priest is still respected
as a man of learning because, even in a highly educated community, he manifestly is one. Sera Benjamin Kristjansson at
Laugaland outside Akuyerí, once priest of Canada's Icelandic
community, with his translations and constant stream of
knowledge-seeking visitors; and Einar Guthnarsson, pastor of
Reykholt, home of Snorri Sturlusson, the poet, whose love of
learning he emulates, as evidenced by his vast collection of
Icelandic folk stories—were among those who gave me, with
unaffected erudition, some of the most illuminating accounts
of Icelandic *mores* I heard. In a different mould there is Parson
Jack, a Scotsman whose influence derives from pastoral care
and involvement in the community. Coming to Iceland to teach
football, he became the first foreign pastor of the Lutheran
Church in modern times, then went off to care for the sixty-
odd chess-playing parishioners of the island of Grimsey isolated
off Iceland's northern coast, and then to Tjörn on a northern
peninsula almost as remote. Parson Jack is one of only half-a-
dozen farming pastors, heirs to the days when a Lutheran
priest was farmer first and pastor second. Such men as these
would be outstanding in any clerical company; yet at
Church headquarters, I had an impression of well-meaning but
drab and uninspiring men, and for all the influence the Church
seemed to have on the fundamentals of Icelandic life today,
one could not but wonder whether the upkeep of its elaborate
machinery by the state was justified.

Iceland consists of a single see, whose bishop has two deputies
who can carry out episcopal duties and cover the old sees of
Holar and Skalholt. These are in turn subdivided into deaneries
and again into nearly 300 parishes which provide livings, in
plurality however, for only some hundred priests. The priests,
who are normally trained at the theological faculty at the

university, are generally elected by the parishioners in the parish they eventually serve. The electorate consists of all parishioners of blameless reputation who are over the age of twenty-one. These priests are, in effect, civil servants, being paid for their services by the government and receiving from their parishioners only the fees for special services, such as weddings and burials. All Icelanders must pay a tithe but may opt for this to be paid to the university rather than the Church, and many take advantage of this option. The pastors have the aid of elected parish councils and themselves meet yearly in synod to discuss organisational and theological problems.

This is a machine without fuel, running on its past impetus, and no one seems able to recall its purpose. From its once positive role, the Church seems to have turned to negativism, to embodying the spirit of 'thou shalt not'. For many Icelanders today, the Church is likely to be thought of more as the vehement—and until recently, successful—champion of prohibition and the temperance movement than as a source of spiritual salvation. No longer is it the best avenue of advancement for the poor intellectual aspiring to an education, and recruitment among the young is slight. Its prospects of regaining its former influence on Icelandic life seem negligible, for, while the Icelanders are a people of great spiritual resources, they have never been fanatical devotees of any particular formalised religion or code of religious practice.

☒

The other estates of the realm, the press (with other communications media) and the trade unions, which move so potently elsewhere, have even less influence on the shape of Icelandic society than the constitutional forces.

The more important of the unofficial establishments is probably the press, in which a running polemical battle is sustained between elections. Yet so exclusively partisan is each newspaper that the collective influence of the press as a whole is vitiated and it cannot be considered as a measure of those swings of public opinion which serve at least as a warning to politicians otherwise immovably entrenched in office.

The oldest extant daily newspaper, started in 1911, is the Reykjavík evening paper *Visir*, which supports the Independence party, as does its stablemate, the morning daily *Morgunblathith*. The latter has a circulation of 36,000, of which 20,000 copies are sold in Reykjavík. The same house publishes a farmers' weekly and a rather cheap Sunday magazine, *Lesbok* (37,000). Thus probably a minimum of three out of four Icelandic readers are subjected daily to the views of the Independence party. The political editor of *Morgunblathith* claims that he is concerned with news while others publish only views. But this is a claim which will be made with equal vehemence by the other leading daily papers. They, however, do not enjoy the added consolation of a dominant circulation since they all come within the 12–18,000 circulation bracket. The Labour party finds its platform in *Althythublathith*, the People's Alliance in *Thjothviljinn* and the Progressives in *Timinn*. There are also a number of equally political local provincial and town papers. All the papers are selective about the news they present and uninhibited in the expression of their views, because they are owned, directed and edited by the political parties and are dependent on the allegiance of political supporters for their guaranteed basic readership. But within that recognised and publicly accepted pattern, they secure a general freedom of the press—whose functions are many other than political, as we shall see in chapter 7—and a public debate of political issues. Even the dominant *Morgunblathith*, with its twenty reporters and eighty stringers (albeit with relatively unsophisticated production plant and single midnight edition press-time), is outnumbered by the combined circulation of the other papers.

The Icelandic press, with its confessed political partisanship, is free to a great extent of the more insidious financial influences which operate behind the front of editorial impartiality in so many Western European newspapers. Advertising accounts for only half of *Morgunblathith*'s revenue, and probably for less with other papers. The remaining income of Icelandic newspapers, other than from party subsidy, is from sales. *Morgunblathith* costs 7 kronur a copy or, more usually, 105 kronur for a monthly subscription. If anything, the press is becoming less partisan, less biased and the readers' letters columns, always open to all, are now being joined by the occasional invited political commentary or feature from a point of view not shared by the editorial board or the party backing it. The Icelandic newspapers, in so many ways comparable with the weekly press in Britain, differ in one marked respect: they give an astonishing coverage of international news. The front pages of the main dailies are often exclusively devoted to foreign news, and an Icelandic event has to be of genuine importance to make the front page. Nevertheless, the Icelandic press is basically little more than the ephemeral paper extension of the political parties. The only exception to this stricture is in its coverage of cultural affairs, to which we shall refer in chapter 7.

One threat the Icelandic press does not yet have to fear is that of television. In 1967, there were only 6,000 television sets in Reykjavík and the surrounding districts, and it is doubtful if, even after completion of the programme for setting up relay stations in the next decade (at a cost of 70–80 million kronur per station), there will ever be more than 30,000 sets or more than twenty-two to twenty-four hours of broadcasting a week. From September 1, 1967, television broadcasting increased from three hours (8 to 11 o'clock in the evening) four times a week to three hours six times a week, but the current debate is not so much about the actual number of hours as about the consequences of extending broadcasting time in terms of programme content and in particular the use of foreign material. British and American programmes can be transmitted at a cost of only a third to a quarter of that of making and transmitting the same amount of home-produced live or video-recorded material.

Development of television has been largely financed by the very high import duties on television sets, but its running costs have in future to come entirely from licence revenue (2,400 kronur annual fee) and the advertising revenue at 9,000 kronur a minute. In 1966, the station was run at a loss of between 2 and 3 million kronur, and it can be seen that, even with extended hours, the revenue ceiling virtually compels Icelanders to get their television on the cheap by importing B-grade programmes from abroad.

The radio service, which is separately run, makes a profit derived from the annual licence fee (620 kronur) paid by each Icelandic household. There cannot be a family in the island, however remotely situated, which does not have a radio set and listen regluarly to one of Europe's oldest services, established in 1930. Licence evasion is impossible since dealers notify the broadcasting authorities of every set sold. In addition, paid advertising brings in some 28 million kronur a year. The radio is a much more impartial medium than either press or television and has built up a reputation akin to that of the British Broadcasting Corporation, from which it derives most of its overseas news. Indeed, its impartiality has even given rise to considerable outbursts of public indignation at such times of high national feeling as the fishing disputes when it gave the British as well as the Icelandic point of view; or more recently, over the appointment of its chief news editor when a man considered insufficiently impartial was obliged to withdraw through public pressure. Of the mass media, radio is still the most influential since its universality and unity are unique in a community with such communication difficulties as Iceland, where the national press has difficulty in reaching remote areas with any degree of immediacy and there is no national television service.

The trade-union movement in Iceland is no more powerful than its sister 'estate' and is itself relatively young. The creation of trade unions was in part delayed by the concentration of economic activity on agriculture until the end of the nineteenth century. The interests of a great part of the rural working population, of which a relatively small number were direct wage-earners as opposed to family dependants, were already protected by the unusual producer-consumer outlook of the co-operatives. Industry, other than fishing, developed slowly; and, until the First World War, fishing was dominated by the small-boat owners whose few crew members were in any case often related. Coupled with the high level of employment until the depression, this meant that there were few real pressures to bring the employed community into organised unions for its own protection. The first union was founded on a very small scale by the sailors and fishermen in 1894. This was followed by the first industrial union in 1896, that of the printers and typographers. The Printers' Union was unusual in two ways: it invited the employers to form a federation with which it could deal, and it operated on a national craft basis from the outset. Otherwise unions in the smaller towns and villages had to embrace a relatively wide range of activities if the membership was ever to reach sufficient size to sustain an effective local organisation. In a few large towns, the unions developed on a craft and occupational basis with a number of varying compromises in different areas between the craft and comprehensive structures. The first unskilled workers union was founded in 1906.

The sparse distribution of population, poor communication and a high level of both job mobility and job multiplicity militated not only against the growth of craft unions but of a trade-union federation. The first abortive attempt to form such a federation was made in 1907. It was restarted in 1916, but, with the birth of a separate Communist party in 1930, ran into trouble and split into two federations in 1938. In

1940, the differences were largely settled between the two groups, and the organisation, now the Icelandic Federation of Labour, was reconstituted. Despite the growth in membership* to an extent that nearly all workers in Iceland are either members of a union affiliated to the Federation or of the Public Employees Union (6,000) or of the Seamen's Officers Union (3,000), the Federation is still an uneasy alliance of widely disparate organisations, some with as few as twenty members. In fact, the union movement in any collective sense has been weakened both by the incessant political manoeuvring within its ranks (although there are only four or five trade-union members of parliament) and by the state of the post-war labour market which has rendered union protection, like unemployment benefit (itself only introduced in 1936), virtually superfluous. The history and the effectiveness of collective bargaining is a good illustration of this.

Collective bargaining has been known in Iceland since 1904, but it was not until 1951 that the Federation negotiated its first collective bargain—and this was little more than a measure consolidating gains already made by individual unions. The Icelandic Federation of Labour is additionally hampered in this context by an aspect of Icelandic union law unique among the Nordic countries whereby the Federation can only make a collective contract binding on those member unions which have specifically asked it to negotiate on their behalf in a given instance. However, collective agreements made by a particular union do take precedence over individual agreements contracted by its members. This lack of control by the Federation is made difficult to rectify by the specific legal protection enjoyed by the shop steward on the spot from even suspected retaliatory action from the employer. He enjoys, for example, preferential treatment during redundancy. He has little to lose, therefore, by bucking the union—let alone the Federation —and plenty to gain from the gratitude of his workmates if he

* 25,000 in 1952; 30,000 in 1957; 34,400 in 133 federated unions in 1966.

gains them better wages or conditions. The union movement labours under the even greater handicap of the inability of its leaders to deliver the goods they promise through lack of control of their own members, both unions and individuals. The exception to this rule comes from the communist-controlled unions which, although they have not regained in the Federation the dominant position they had in the 1940s, are still the most cohesive single force in the movement. If a communist union enters into an agreement, it is kept. We thus find the ironic situation in which both employers and capitalist-orientated government prefer to deal with their nominal arch-enemies in the interests of a well-ordered and disciplined labour market. There is, in fact, no formal machinery for consulting the unions, but the government keeps in close unofficial liaison.

There is, however, an elaborate machinery for the conduct of industrial disputes, which have become increasingly frequent since the war, and for attempts to avoid them. The right to strike is constitutionally guaranteed, but it is hedged about with certain provisions. Political strikes are illegal, as are those in breach of contract. The Labour Court, set up in 1938, consisting of two Supreme Court judges and a representative each of the Icelandic Federation of Labour, the employers and the Ministry of Social Security, is charged with interpreting contracts and adjudicating on charges of breach of contract. It awards damages to the employers according to the loss or damage they have sustained as a result of illegal work stoppages. The court is also responsible for interpreting and enforcing the laws governing the rights and conduct of the trade unions themselves, and it acts, if it agrees to do so, as arbitrator when called on by contending parties. But the Labour Court is intended as a last resort. In 1925, a mediation system was created; its present operative form dates from 1938, when a mediator was appointed for each of the four regions of Iceland. (The Reykjavík mediator acts also as state mediator.) Would-be strikers have to notify both their employers and the mediator of their intention to withdraw labour seven days before they do so. The mediator has to try to reconcile the parties by means of both separate and joint meetings held in private and in the strictest confidence. If he fails in this, and industrial action is taken, he then publishes the facts of the dispute, as he, and he alone, interprets them, so that the public may decide for itself where it thinks justice in the quarrel lies.

The individual employee is in a very strong position in Iceland today and in most cases probably pays his union dues (one-sixth of a man's standard day's pay per week, one-ninth of the male day's wage for women) purely as an insurance against a return to the high unemployment level of the 1930s. If he has a row with his boss and walks out or gets thrown out of his job, he can so easily go one hundred yards down the road and obtain an equally well-paid one that he does not often think it worth involving his workmates in a strike over his personal grievance. If he does find himself in a strike, it will almost certainly be one of unions versus employers and state over price and wage-fixing, inflation or some other national economic consideration. While such strikes can be interpreted as political and a technical breach of the constitution, it would be impossible and probably unwise to try to penalise those involved. With the growing appreciation by union officials of the nature of Iceland's economic problems, such action will probably diminish. Short of an economic collapse, the trade-union movement is likely to have only a marginal use as a sounding-board and safety-valve in the immediate future.

❦

We can see from the institutions examined in this chapter that those forces which have done so much to shape other European societies are of lesser importance in Iceland. Institutions and organisations either serve as vehicles for the expression of privately and previously formulated opinions, as do the press and the Althing, or act as indicators, like Church, law and unions, of the marked lack of neuroses and tensions in Icelandic society. It is as an indicator rather than an influence that we must also examine Iceland's relations with the outside world. While its relationship with Denmark, the colonial power, did much to shape its outlook until the Second World War, its post-war conduct of international affairs appears to be symptomatic of an attitude already inherent in the Icelandic character.

6

The 'Cod War' and International Relations

ROUND the deadly coasts of Iceland, in places remote from human habitation and often even from the simplest dirt road, stands a picket line of wooden huts. They are survival huts. On the food and fuel stored in them may depend the life of any lucky survivor who makes the shore from one of the endless shipwrecks in Icelandic coastal waters. When Harry Eddom, sole survivor of the *Ross Cleveland*, the British trawler which sank in a few seconds one February day in 1968 off Isafjord, struggled ashore to find shelter and a quick-thinking farm boy, he was neither Icelander nor Englishman, just another less unlucky victim of the seas' cold impartiality. The *Ross Cleveland* had become helplessly encrusted with ice, one of the many perils in Icelandic waters, and turned turtle. It was not the only tragedy at that time, for two other British trawlers also went down, with a loss of fifty-eight lives. People sitting in the comfort of their homes in Britain were aghast—and perhaps, momentarily, grateful that they did not have to earn a living in so tough a way.

It *is* a tough way to earn a living, yet most of those who follow it would have no other. And the British deep-sea fisherman does at least have a choice: he can move into one of a thousand other well-paid jobs in Britain's complex, if not always very healthy, economy. The Icelandic fisherman generally does not have such a choice, particularly if he does not sail from Reykjavík but from one of the northern or eastern ports. There, if he does not work on a fishing vessel, he may not work at all.

In Britain, the fishing industry is an important sector of the economy, not only in terms of the livelihood of those communities in Hull, Grimsby and Aberdeen which depend on it, but nationally.

In 1948 and 1952, when there occurred the earliest rumblings of the fishing-limits dispute between the two nations, Britain was suffering from the first of those post-war balance-of-payments crises which have plagued it ceaselessly ever since. At the time of the worst conflict in 1958, the value of the fishing industry's catch was equivalent to a saving in foreign exchange large enough to pay for the entire 55,000-strong British forces in Germany. The prospect of substantial losses of a commodity which would have to be made good in foreign exchange could not, therefore, be regarded lightly. But if the fishing industry was important to Britain, it was vital to Iceland. Iceland's problem was not simply serious but absolute.

After centuries of poverty, the Icelandic people were enjoying in the post-war period the standards of living of the very rich nations. As we saw in chapter 4, those standards of living depended entirely on the nation's capacity to buy industrial and consumer goods with money earned almost exclusively by the fishing industry. The fortunes of war had enabled Iceland to make the economic breakthrough to prosperity. Poverty the Icelanders understood and had endured. They could doubtless have continued to endure it as stoically had their fortunes not improved. But to obtain undreamed-of material wealth in less than a decade and then to see the threat of its abrupt withdrawal as other fishing fleets returned to the seas round the coast of their country—this was more than Icelanders could be expected to bear calmly and purely rationally.

An understanding of these psychological factors and an appreciation of the role of fishing in maintaining Iceland's new prosperity is essential to any judgement of its attitudes and conduct in the extension of its territorial waters and fishing limits. The British public has largely been aware of Iceland only in the context of fishing disputes and the action it has taken in them. Moreover, while appreciating that fishing is important to Iceland, the British public has had little idea of just how important it really is.

⊠

The strength of Icelandic feeling dates back to the island's earliest days as a Danish colony, when Denmark became responsible for its external affairs and hence for the protection of its territorial waters. At the turn of the twentieth century, this function of the colonial power became particularly important to the nascent modern Icelandic fishing industry. One of Iceland's most heartfelt grievances against Denmark was its lack of concern for the island's fishing interests. Iceland had more to complain about than just neglect for, by a treaty with Britain in 1901, Denmark virtually connived at the exploitation of Iceland's coastal waters by British vessels. The principal feature of the treaty was Danish recognition that the British concept of territorial waters—and hence at this time fishing limits—as three miles from the low-water mark shore-line applied to Iceland. This opened Iceland's bays, hitherto largely protected by much more extensive (if admittedly diminishing) traditional limits, to British trawlermen. In the first decade of this century, when Iceland's small-boat fishing industry was reaching take-off point and before it had developed its own trawler fleet to any extent, British trawlers, ostensibly acting within the terms of the treaty, were not only fishing in vast numbers all round the three-mile limit but many times a day crossing it with impunity and going right up into the fjords and bays where the young fish bred. Often the Icelanders' gear was ruined by these British vessels and the damage to their fishing was enormous. Not that the harm was all of foreign origin: the sight of a row of Icelandic boats strung across the mouth of a fjord, their nets thus virtually blocking off the sea from the young fish, was by no means uncommon.

With the coming of the Second World War and the confident approach of independence, these grievances against Denmark and Britain diminished in importance for a while. But in 1944, the very year of independence, the herring shoals suddenly swam away again. Not surprisingly, the Icelanders turned their minds to the conservation and maintenance of the white-fish stocks which, left to breed and multiply in peace during the war, were subjected after 1945 to an almost militarily mounted harassment with the return of peace and the rush of foreign vessels back to the rich banks. The first protective step taken by the Icelanders was in 1948 when they initiated some minor conservation measures, including some modest adjustments of the coastal areas closed to foreign fishing vessels. These measures met with protest from both the British trawler owners and the Foreign Office; but, since they impinged but little on an industry which was itself still rebuilding after the war, the protest was taken no further. It was soon apparent, however, that these minor adjustments were inadequate to secure for Iceland the degree of protection it was seeking.

In May 1952, Iceland extended its fishing limits over an area four miles out to sea from a baseline drawn from headland to headland. This replaced the three-mile line which, with the exception of a number of large bays claimed in 1948, was in general based on the low-water mark of the main shoreline. The decision to make this extension was largely prompted by the International Court of Justice's ruling (December 18, 1951) on the dispute between Britain and Norway over the latter's fishing zone. An examination of this important legal case does much to explain the attitudes subsequently adopted by Britain and Iceland during the 1950s, when they were involved in a continuous series of similar disagreements.

The quarrel between Britain and Norway began in 1906, when British fishing vessels ventured for the first time into waters off the Norwegian coast which the Norwegians had hitherto regarded, without dispute, as their own exclusive preserve. On July 12, 1935, the government in Oslo published a decree delimiting its fishing zone as the area four miles (one Norwegian nautical mile) beyond a baseline drawn through the 'rock rampart', including islands, islets, rocks and reefs, rather than beyond a baseline contiguous to the mainland. The dispute was not so much about the change from a three- to a four-mile limit as about the baseline from which it was drawn. The war temporarily suspended the argument but it was hotly resumed in 1948–49, when the Norwegian authorities arrested a large number of British fishing vessels which considered themselves to be still on the high seas. Britain referred the matter to the International Court and Norway agreed to abide by its decision. The importance Britain attached to the court's impending judgement was made clear by the attorney-general, Sir Frank Soskice, when he opened the British case.

It is not only a very important one to the United Kingdom and to Norway, but the decision on it will be of the very greatest importance to the world generally as a precedent, because the court's decision in this case must contain important pronouncements regarding the rules of international

law relating to coastal waters ... the court will see that it is
not Norway's title to her fjords or to the waters inside her
groups of islands and outside the limit of her fjords and sounds
that are in dispute. It is the baselines, some of them of great
length, to which the United Kingdom is objecting, lines
drawn along the outside of the coast and outside the fringe
of islands, because it is the use of these baselines that Norway
claims to exclude the fishermen of all other countries from
fishing in areas which appear to the United Kingdom at all
events, to be obviously the high seas.[1]

Britain's historical commitment to maximum freedom of the
high seas has always been an important part of its arguments
in all disputes concerning territorial waters. Although its own
three-mile limit is determined by the range of an eighteenth-
century cannon shot from the shore, it has resisted all subsequent temptations to extend it. Cynics might retort that this
apparent self-denying ordinance is, in fact, prompted by the
same considerations which Lord Salisbury had in mind when
rejecting a Dutch proposal for the extension of territorial waters
at the end of the nineteenth century. The Dutch pointed out
that, with such an extensive coastline, Britain itself had most to
gain. Lord Salisbury replied: 'However extensive ours may be,
the fish are found on yours.' Nevertheless, a genuine commitment to the fullest navigational freedom was part of the
British case against both Norway and Iceland.

The Norwegian case at The Hague was based on a combination of geographical, historical and social factors rather than
on legal interpretations and precedents, which in any case
seemed to be imprecise in this matter. The coastline of Norway
is almost unique and, the Norwegians argued, could only be
properly defined by the inclusion of all those rocky outcrops in
the sea whose size was immaterial provided they were within
sight of the mainland. The livelihood of the coastal population
depended on the waters in dispute in which they had fished

without competition until the twentieth century. In the words of one of the advocates for Norway: 'If you take away from these people their fishing banks, you take away their soil.'[2]

The International Court found unequivocally (ten to two) in Norway's favour. It based its decision on a complete acceptance of the three points, geographical, historical and social, on which the Norwegian claim was based. The court's judgement also made it clear that, while the case could be considered as setting certain precedents, these were dependent on particular circumstances, and that disputes over fishing limits in the future were the proper subject of international law and not unilateral, arbitrary decisions. British apprehension was expressed by the dissenting British judge, Sir Arnold McNair. In his opinion:

> The manipulation of the limits of territorial waters for the purpose of protecting economic and other social interests has no justification in law; moreover, the approbation of such practice would have a dangerous tendency, in that it would encourage states to adopt a subjective appreciation of their rights instead of conforming to a common international standard. In these circumstances, I consider the delimitation of territorial waters made by the Norwegian decree of 1935 is in conflict with international law, and that its effects will be to injure the principle of freedom of the seas and encourage further encroachments upon the high seas by coastal states.[3]

Sir Arnold did not know how soon his prediction was to come true. Even so, despite the fact that the British government did not concur with the judgement, it expressed its willingness to abide by the court's decision and, indeed, confirmed its faith in international law as the sole proper means of settling such disputes.

It is this British attitude which makes the Icelanders' subsequent conduct of their dispute with Britain, if not its objectives, so surprising. There can be little doubt that, in acting on the Norwegian precedent (on which, in fact, it did base its claims in

1952), Iceland would have had a very strong case in international law. Had it been prepared to go to The Hague, it would almost certainly have obtained a no less favourable judgement than Norway. Iceland's coastline is one of the few comparable with Norway's; and if the historical claims were weaker in that British vessels had fished off the Icelandic coast for more than five centuries, the social grounds, to which the International Court had attached so much importance, were far stronger. In Iceland's case it was not the livelihood of a coastal community which appeared to be threatened but that of a whole people.

Yet, neither at the outset of the 1952 dispute, nor when subsequently invited by the British government, would the Icelandic government submit to the jurisdiction of the International Court, although it did press its case in a number of international bodies such as NATO and OECD, to which both it and Britain belonged. Although the British commercial interests involved were far larger than they had been in the Norwegian case, there was nothing in Britain's conduct which could justifiably have led Iceland to suppose that it would ignore a court decision unfavourable to its interests. Such was the anxiety of the Icelanders over the preservation, as they saw it, of their national livelihood that they were not even prepared to run the risk of putting a good case to the hazard of law. Moreover, they denied that the extension was anything but a domestic matter.

The British Foreign Office immediately protested against the Icelandic extension, as did the governments of Belgium, France and the Netherlands. The protests were ignored. British trawler skippers and crews expressed their objections in more concrete form by threatening to go on strike if any Icelandic fish were landed in Britain when their trawlers were being barred from Icelandic waters in which they had previously fished. The trawler owners endorsed the seamen's attitude and imposed a total ban on the landing of Icelandic fish which was to cost

Iceland some £2 million a year. They were able to do this—as they still can—not by law but by virtue of the fact that they own among them all the equipment necessary for the unloading and handling of the fish. Despite appeals from the government in Reykjavík, the British government refused to intervene to prevent the ban, on the grounds that it was powerless to do so. In any case, the Conservative administration then in office, and still feeling its way after six years in opposition, clearly sympathised with the trawler owners and endorsed the stand taken by its Labour predecessor on the principle of limiting territorial waters to three miles.

The British trawler owners now turned their attention to more distant and costly waters. A crack appeared in their front in October 1953 when one owner, George Dawson, backed by a number of small fish merchants who were feeling the lack of Icelandic fish, began to take landings. But his bid to beat the restrictions did not last long, not least because, as a single owner, he could not come to terms with the Icelandic trawler owners, who did not seem greatly to care at the time whether he accepted their fish or not. Unofficial overtures from the trawler owners were as unacceptable as official government approaches to the Icelanders, who were even more determined to accept no compromise.

The quarrel dragged on until November 1956, when an unofficial group set up by the Organisation for European Economic Co-operation (now the Organisation for Economic Co-operation and Development) on the initiative of the two fishing industries managed to persuade the British to agree to the resumption of landings. This concession was to be without prejudice to Britain's legal stand or the conclusions which might be reached at the forthcoming Geneva conference on the law of the sea. The total of Icelandic landings, moreover, was not to exceed an annual value of £1·8 million. Iceland, in return, would allow British trawlers to run for port in foul weather without having completely to stow their fishing gear.

137

(They had previously been required to cut loose their gear when seeking shelter, and this regulation had caused the vessels considerable loss.)

The practical effect of the 1952 extension of the Icelandic fishing limit on the British fishing industry seems to have been minimal. Apart from a slight drop in catch in 1952, the tonnage obtained by British trawlers rose rapidly and in 1953 was half as much again as the 1951 figure (see Table 9, page 206). The main impact, in fact, was on Iceland's over-all trading pattern. Between 1951 and 1954, both the value of Icelandic fish products to Britain* and of its imports from Britain was halved. In the same period, Russia, which had had no trade in either direction since 1948, developed both imports and exports (mainly petroleum and vehicles) of about £3 million with Iceland. This trend roused considerable fears in some quarters in Britain that Russia was intending to exploit Iceland's desperate need of alternative markets in order to prise it loose from NATO and strengthen its Communist party. In the event, these fears proved quite unfounded, and the main result of the landing ban was to encourage the Icelandic fish-processing industry to improve both quantitively and qualitatively and to seek new markets. It should also be emphasised that the new fishing limits were applied in general to Icelandic as well as to foreign trawlers (but not to line-fishing vessels whose catch, from being substantially less than that of the trawlers, temporarily increased in the following year). Iceland was quite genuinely concerned with the conservation of fishing stocks rather than with the opportunity to make quick profits at other nations' expense. Not to have expressed this concern in practical measures would have been unthinkable.

⬗

But the disagreement between the two countries was not resolved by the 1956 agreement. During the 1950s, the Icelanders

* Packaged frozen fish was not affected by the trawler owners' ban.

became increasingly anxious about overfishing: an anxiety regarded as exaggerated by the British fishing industry. The British maintained that the 1953–56 catch was disproportionately inflated by the maturing of the particularly large young cod 'class' of 1945 and the decrease in the size of net-meshes. This, however, was not how the Icelanders saw it. To them, the temporary upsurge was due to the 1952 extension of limits. They had no doubt that their future was being jeopardised by overfishing. In 1957–58, matters came to a head on two fronts. The fish catch off Iceland's coasts fell sharply again and the Geneva conference on the law of the sea proved as abortive as many had feared. By itself, the fall in the total whitefish catch would have proved nothing for it might, for example, have reflected one of the cyclical upsurges in herring-fishing activity but the catch, even by British figures, also fell between 12 and 35 per cent throughout the various fishing fleets in terms of the units of effort involved, measured in man-fishing hours (see Table 10).

The Geneva conference produced only a mass of conflicting legal opinions and suggestions about fishing limits. Britain, while advocating the retention of the old three miles, was prepared to concede six; Canada suggested a twelve-mile fishing limit; Russia proposed variable limits between three and twelve miles; the United States supported the Canadian suggestion, with an amendment allowing special rights for traditional fishers of from six to twelve miles. Iceland supported the twelve-mile limit, but, when this failed to gain acceptance, proposed preferential rights outside the lesser limits for nations dependent on coastal fishing. The conflicts of view were unresolved (the American proposal coming closest to gaining the necessary two-thirds majority), and the conference broke up with agreement on nothing but the need to reconvene at a future date (1960).

Iceland therefore decided to take matters into its own hands without further delay and announced, as it had hinted in 1952, an extension of fishing limits to twelve miles from the 1952 baseline as from September 1, 1958. This was a much more serious blow to Britain than the 1952 extension, for now 20 to 25 per cent of its total fish catch was involved, with the prospect of the haul of cod, halibut, plaice, etc., being halved.

The British government entered the dispute immediately and vigorously protested at the extension, as did the other major fishing nations. This time, however, it went further and thus placed itself as far beyond international law as had the government of Iceland by its decision. The Icelanders were bluntly told that British trawlers would ignore the limit and that the Royal Navy would ensure that they were not arrested by Icelandic fishery-protection vessels for doing so. Britain argued that the total fish catch involved had doubled in the period from 1936–38 to 1953–55; while Iceland's share of it had risen from 31 to 48 per cent, that of Britain and Germany, the two principal foreign fleets involved, had declined by 12 and 3 per cent respectively. (Reykjavík sources give the Icelandic increase as being from 31 to 45 per cent, and the British and German decline as by 11 and 1 per cent respectively; but the general case is not in dispute.) The British, while understandably indignant, thus showed in their reply that they had missed the point of the Icelandic claim. The increase in catch size of the order experienced reinforced the suggestion that the area was being overfished.

Attempts were made through NATO to avert the impending physical confrontation of the two allies, but these were not helped by the British suspicion of the fact that the Icelandic minister for Fisheries was a member of the Communist party, which was then a member of the coalition government. Subsequently, the British government proposed two compromises: a maximum catch to be agreed for the area, of which between one-half and two-thirds would be allocated to Iceland with, in addition, some zones reserved exclusively for its line fishermen; or a selective extension of the limits in those areas most important to Iceland. While the first alternative was a conservationist one, but offering little prospect of agreement on what constituted a safe level of fishing, the second had the appearance of being designed to trap the Icelanders into the admission of non-conservationist motives for extending the limits by another eight miles. Reykjavík insisted that the position was not negotiable. Nor was there any way in which both parties could be reconciled by a decision of the International Court, for as long as Iceland refused to acknowledge its jurisdiction, Britain's proposal to take the matter there could not in any way be enforced.

From September 1, 1958, Iceland sought to impose its new limits by the exercise of force while Britain prevented it from doing so by exercising superior force in what many people regarded as one of the worst cases of international bullying, short of armed conflict, since the Second World War. The real tragedy, however, was that two close former friends should each be unshakably convinced, from diametrically opposed points of view, of its own rectitude. Between September 1, 1958, and June 28, 1960, seventy unsuccessful attempts were made to arrest British trawlers. Blank shots, and some live rounds across the bows, were exchanged, and the British trawlermen defended, or threatened to defend, themselves with knives, axes, hot irons and boiling water hoses and by trying to ram the Icelandic vessels. The main British tactic, however, was to use the greater size and speed of the Royal Navy's frigates to interpose them between the trawlers and the six small Icelandic fishery-protection vessels. It is a tribute to the seamanship and commonsense of the men on the spot that in all this time there was only one minor collision. When the Icelanders did get a boarding party on a trawler, they were removed by armed force to an RN frigate. There they spent several amicable days when their parent ship refused to take them back, on the grounds that they should be returned to the trawler. They were then surreptitiously put ashore in the dead of night, presumably so that the frigate would not be liable to arrest if caught in Icelandic waters. So the tragi-comedy was played out.

Meanwhile, the verbal battle went on. The British popular press endorsed the navy's actions, while the Icelandic embassy in London went so far beyond the niceties of diplomatic protocol as to distribute a booklet entitled *British Aggression in Icelandic Waters*, giving a trenchant summary of the Icelandic legal, economic and diplomatic case. Exaggeration was rife on both sides. Thor Thors at the United Nations (to which both sides submitted memoranda[4] which might almost have been on different topics!) described Britain's past conduct thus: 'Swarms of British trawlers have scraped the bottom of the sea almost up to the door of our poor fishermen's homes.' This was certainly laying it on rather thick for the benefit of his audience, but accusations in the British press of virtual piracy and piscine imperialism were no less far-fetched. I was a newspaper leader-writer in Britain at the time and remember the difficulty I had in persuading my normally most reasonable editor that this was not a case to be argued on the niceties of international law (in which, in any case, the Icelanders had a strong argument) but rather on the grounds of natural justice; that however intransigently the Icelanders had put forward their claim, it was one with which we ought to sympathise because the ensuring of good fish stocks for the future was their only way of ensuring their future livelihood.

In the meanwhile, Britain had protestingly acquiesced when Denmark (around the Faroes) and Russia each unilaterally created twelve-mile limits which the British still regard as illegal. The Icelanders were quick to point out that these were countries on which the British were less anxious to try gun-boat diplomacy. The second Geneva conference on the law of the sea was called for April 1960. Although, like the first, it reached no agreed conclusions, it did provide an opportunity for the dispute between Britain and Iceland to be resolved. As a gesture of good will, the British trawler owners withdrew from the new Icelandic waters for the duration of the conference and when it ended extended the truce for a further three months. Some trawlers ignored the truce but those that did were punished by the British Trawler Federation by being suspended from fishing. In any case, by the late summer of 1960 the trawlers were without the continual mothering of the Royal Navy and the protected 'fishing boxes' it had created. The Icelanders, in turn, agreed to suspend all attempts to land fish in Britain. (During this 1958–60 dispute, there had been no attempt at a comprehensive landing ban, for the British trawler owners had found it to be an ineffectual weapon against the Icelandic economy on the previous occasion.)

Official talks between the two sides were begun in October 1960 after a further Anglo–Norwegian fishing agreement on Norway's similar extension. This had given Britain fishing rights between the six- and twelve-mile limits for a phase-out period of ten years. The Anglo–Icelandic talks yielded some minor Icelandic concessions but were otherwise a complete victory for Iceland. The baselines were redrawn in its favour. British trawlers were to have rights for only three years in about one-third of the newly protected waters, whereas Norway, which had not quibbled at the extension, was to enjoy them for ten years. Iceland agreed to give six months' notice of any future alterations and, most important, to submit to the ruling of the International Court any disputes which might subsequently arise.

Grudgingly, on March 10, 1961, the British trawler owners accepted the settlement. Only the skippers and crews have remained aggrieved and unreconciled, but their animosity has been largely dispelled over the past few years by the heroic efforts of Icelanders on a number of occasions to save the lives of British crews in trouble off the Icelandic coast.

Since 1961, the agreement has generally worked well. The drop in the British catch was initially of the order of 15 to 20 per cent, but advances in trawler design and the introduction of factory ships have partly offset this. Although there has been a steady sequence of infringements of the new limits by British trawlers, these have been subject, without interference, to Icelandic law. The most notorious incident was that involving Captain Newton of the Grimsby trawler *Brandur* who, when arrested in 1967 and held for trial in Reykjavík, calmly sailed out of the harbour with two embarrassed policemen on board without anyone being any the wiser. He was subsequently made to return and convicted, given a prison sentence of six months (from which he was shortly reprieved) and fined 400,000 kronur.

There is no doubt that the 1961 settlement was a resounding success for Icelandic diplomacy, whatever face-saving minor concessions were extracted by the British. Yet, surprisingly, if one does not take account of the Icelandic temperament, it was not greeted with unalloyed enthusiasm in Iceland. Criticism was largely directed at the clause agreeing to submit future disputes to the International Court and was based on the contention that all such matters were of purely national concern. Certainly, the prospect is remote of getting the International Court to endorse Iceland's ultimate ambition (confessed personally to the author by the present prime minister, Bjarni Benediksson) of acquiring exclusive rights over the whole continental shelf. Even the most far-reaching advocacy by any other nation has hitherto been limited to a twelve-mile claim. The criticism of the clause agreeing to international jurisdiction originated within the opposition Progressive and People's Alliance parties. One spokesman described the agreement as 'the greatest national shame and a disgraceful renunciation of the nation's legal rights!' On the other hand, the then prime minister, Olafur Thors, described the settlement as 'a bright honour to Britain', which showed it 'to be a great power with the honesty to give a small neighbour an honest solution'. How permanent a solution this will be in the light of Iceland's long-term ambitions remains to be seen. The present prime minister insisted to me most strongly that any further extension would be entirely in accordance with international law; but, as we have seen, 'international law' is open to a wide variety of interpretations.

There are several lessons to be learned from the decade of disagreement between these two old friends. One certainly seems to be that the risk of any recurrence of the misunderstanding could be diminished if Britain were both to help Iceland to diversify its economy (and thus become less naturally obsessive about its dependence on fish), and also to ease—as far as it lies in Britain's limited power—its passage and conditions of entry into those international economic groupings in Europe to which Britain either belongs or is seeking admission. It was not, I think, ever appreciated by the British, taking home their six penn'orth of fish wrapped in some journal demanding retribution against Iceland, that maintaining a high level of fish catch was the only way for Iceland to maintain a reasonable standard of living and avoid a return to the abysmal poverty of its recent past. There are men alive in Iceland today who have endured times compared with which Britain during the pre-war depression enjoyed an age of affluence. Nor was it realised that without economic independence the Icelanders feared that they would lose all the national identity which they so treasured.

⊠

The Icelandic attitude to foreigners is slightly ambivalent. As individuals, foreigners are welcomed with great friendliness, hospitality and curiosity; collectively, they represent, even if only at the subconscious level, a threat to national identity. This ambivalence is evident in Iceland's attitude to the growing economic communities of Europe.

Apart from its membership of NATO, the only regional group

to which Iceland belongs* is the Nordic Union, which cannot be described in any practical sense as a tightly knit organisation. The Union is the development of the close, if ever-shifting, relationships over the centuries of the five countries of Scandinavia, or Norden as they prefer to call it. Once the problems of individual national independence had been at least temporarily solved by Norway's withdrawal from the union with Sweden in 1905, by Finland's escape from the tyranny of Russian rule during the October Revolution in 1917 and Iceland's attainment of home rule in the following year, the five countries (Denmark being the other) were able to contemplate a looser voluntary association. However, though the First World War drew them closer together, the Second World War found the countries of Norden on all three sides, Allied, Axis and neutral, and they were thus unable to resolve their differences over defence and alliances when the conflict was over. Sweden adhered to its neutrality; Denmark and Norway, with bitter memories of their unpreparedness and subsequent sufferings in 1940, joined NATO, as did Iceland; Finland, involved in three wars within five years, could not escape the implications of its conflicts with and proximity to the Soviet Union and was compelled to follow a special brand of neutrality within the Russian sphere of influence.

Nevertheless, in 1953, the Nordic Council, excluding Finland, was formed and the latter country joined in 1955 with the proviso of self-exclusion from all joint military discussions or action. Despite the regular attendance of prime ministers and foreign ministers, the Nordic Union is still largely all things to all men. Hence Iceland does not have the experience—its practical involvement in NATO being so limited—of belonging to a supranational body demanding any real relinquishment of sovereignty.

This is not to say that many politicians and businessmen have

* At the time of writing, that is; but see page 148 below in regard to Iceland's application to join EFTA.

not appreciated the advantages to be gained (or rather the dis-
advantages to be avoided) by membership of just such a body,
EFTA, of which its partners in the Nordic Union and one of
its chief trading partners, Britain, form the substance. The
temptations to join came largely from the desire for equal competition, with Norway especially, in selling fish to traditional
Icelandic markets, particularly to Britain, in which the
members of EFTA enjoy increasing low-tariff advantages.
Strangely enough, while most members of EFTA feel that its
failure to progress further in terms of economic and political
unity, either alone or as part of the European Economic
Community, will be its main disadvantage, the danger
as far as Iceland is concerned is precisely the possibility
that such a partnership might entail a greater surrender of
sovereignty than the Althing or the people could countenance.

The advantages of a measure of external tariff protection
and of low internal tariffs with a 'home' market reckoned in
hundreds of millions rather than the mere two hundred
thousand or so consumers that Iceland has at present would
seem, superficially, to make membership of the EEC itself an
even more attractive proposition. This is particularly true now
that other fishing nations of Europe, despite Britain's failure to
gain admission to EEC, seem to have much improved chances
of a successful application for full or associate membership.
Yet such advantages, however tempting and whatever the route
possible to obtain them, certainly involve three considerations
intolerable to the Icelanders: the right of member countries
of the EEC to fish within each other's limits, the free movement
of labour, and the free movement of capital. It is the latter two
fundamental considerations of the Rome Treaty whose fulfil-
ment would cause the real nightmare to Iceland. It was bad
enough having 7,000 American servicemen at Keflavík—
equivalent to 4 per cent of the population; they at least could
be safely walled up in the camp. But any influx of poor Euro-
peans could, in a couple of generations, completely obliterate

the small and sexually easy-going Icelandic population. Foreign capital, too, would pose a threat for it would almost certainly be attracted to the sacred fishing industry on which Iceland is so dependent. The Icelanders' attitude to foreign capital is sensibly relaxed as far as other sectors of industry are concerned: but they have a very real fear of the domination and, so to speak, 'alienation' of the fishing industry by foreign interests.

The terms of any form of membership of EEC which would satisfy the Icelanders' need for special safeguards would be so narrow as to render association valueless from the Community's point of view, unless they were seen as part of the general move towards a much wider European economic and political regrouping. Certainly, full membership of the EEC under the terms of the Rome Treaty would be totally unacceptable to Iceland. Hence its reluctance even to join EFTA lest at any time this merged collectively with the EEC and, compelled to withdraw, the Icelanders found themselves even worse off than before. However, in January 1969, Iceland made formal application to join EFTA, for it can no longer afford to remain in isolation from Western Europe. We have already seen the effects of inflation on its export prices, particularly outside the fishing industry whose own vulnerability has been emphasised by steep and steady price falls in both 1967 and 1968. To cope with the price falls, the only steps Iceland has been able to take have been the 24·6 devaluation of 1967 and a further drastic devaluation of 35·2 per cent in November 1968, aimed at boosting the volume of exports beyond the break-even point in terms of their declining value. The measure of Iceland's problem and the need for it to gain admission to a strong economic group, able to sustain a reasonable price level for its exports, can be seen from the fact that the fall in the value of its exports in 1967 was 35 per cent; and, despite the devaluation which it was hoped would lift exports by 10 per cent, there has been in 1968 a further decline of 15 per cent on the 1966 level.

It remains to be seen whether the existing members of EFTA, with their own vociferous fishing communities, will welcome Iceland in exchange for its small market for their industrial goods, particularly as Iceland has asked for a ten-year transition period and the continuance of its bilateral arrangements (including a Soviet petrol and oil monopoly) with Russia. However, it is to be hoped that EFTA, and Britain as the strongest partner therein, will take a more generous view than purely commercial considerations might dictate.

On the imports side, Iceland can do little more to reduce their volume by raising its tariffs; and it can resort to quota restrictions only in so far as these are compatible with its subscription (in 1964) to the General Agreement on Tariffs and Trade (GATT). Since 1963, Iceland has, in fact, made large reductions in its tariff barriers and quota restrictions. The then prevailing maximum tariff of 300 per cent has been reduced to 125 per cent and duties on many specific commodities have been cut. Nevertheless, on some categories of goods they remain high.* In many instances this high duty has been intended to discourage the import of luxury goods (with little success); but in some others, as with the 65 per cent wool and synthetic textile duty, they have given a misleading degree of protection to domestic industries which renders them weak in the export markets of Europe. With its present tax structure, however, it would be unreasonable to expect the Icelandic government to lower duties by much, even were the economic climate favourable, for they represent a very large part of government revenue (see Table 17).

The alternative for Iceland to developing a place in European markets is to expand fish sales to the United States where, although tariffs are progressively higher, a chain of Icelandic processing plants has grown up behind the tariff lines.

---

* For example: cars, 90 per cent plus luxury taxes, making a total of 200 per cent of c.i.f. value; radio and TV, 80 per cent; wool and synthetic textiles, 65 per cent; trucks, 40 per cent.

Otherwise it must look to the Soviet Union and the Eastern bloc, hitherto not very satisfactory trading partners, but better than no market at all. It would be a great pity if necessity compelled Iceland to depend extensively on trade with the Eastern bloc, for which the *quid pro quo* might be distasteful to the West, or exclusively on trade with the United States, which would erode its independence.

The consequences of Iceland's continued economic isolation and the collapse of its fish exporting are alarming, and its people will either have to face up to drastic changes in their tax structure, trading pattern and the rate of improvement in their living standards, or seriously contemplate losing part of that national sovereignty and independence they hold so dear. It is small wonder in such a situation that Iceland is so sensitive about its fishing limits or that it is prepared to act in ways which may seem unreasonable to other nations.

The fishing dispute merits an examination for more than just its illustration of Iceland's economic dilemma. It also highlights certain distinctive Icelandic characteristics. The Icelanders felt that they were justified morally, legally and by the necessities of survival in the action they took. Having reached this conclusion, they pursued it with ruthless logic and unshakable resolution, accepting all the consequences of defying a great naval power and major customer. They won their goals by their persistence and must, therefore, look on their actions as additionally justified by success. The independence shown by the Icelandic people as a whole was the collective extension of the personal independence and individual freedom so sacred to them.

Whether in a world of increasing interdependence such national individualism can survive is open to doubt, but Iceland's admirers must hope so; and any country which would be friends must remain in no doubt as to the sole terms on which such friendship can be obtained. This obsession with independence is national, economic, cultural, social and even ethnic.

It gives Iceland enormous strength but sometimes renders it inflexible. Yet this independence, this passionate patriotism, is of a rare kind in that it is entirely lacking in xenophobia. At no time during their dispute did the Icelanders condemn or hate the British, collectively or as individuals. All that was condemned were the *actions* of the British government. This ability to distinguish between an idea or policy and the human beings implementing it is rare in any context, let alone in international politics. But if independence is so signal an Icelandic virtue, whence do its people derive the inner certainty which enables them to refuse any compromise, even in the face of the longest odds?

7

The Last Civilisation

Fortunate island,
Where all men are equal
But not vulgar—not yet.
W. H. Auden, *Iceland Revisited*

THE ICELANDERS have been both inspired and shackled by their 'Golden Age': inspired to an unshakable belief in the value of intellectual and spiritual accomplishment, even in the midst of oppressive poverty; shackled by the consequent belief that any creations, customs or occupations which depart from the forms, one might even say formulae, of that Golden Age are to that degree lower in standard, less worthy of a true man.

This mood is captured by the organist in Halldor Laxness's novel, *The Atom Station*: 'We have been rather an insignificant nation, except that we wrote this heroic literature seven hundred years ago.' There is a suggestion of an unquestioned greatness in that literature on which the men of subsequent ages, until the last war, built with equal certainty a belief in their own national greatness. The nations whose literature and language is of Germanic origin, having no classical literature of their own, have since subscribed no less unquestioningly to the same hagiology. In Laxness's own words: 'We had something which the Germanic world did not have, classical literature. This is what we lived on and nothing else.'[1]

Yet this same pride seems able to engender, sometimes even in a writer of Laxness's stature, a despair of ever being able to emulate the writers of that classical age. A look of genuine regret, almost satisfied regret, crosses his face for a moment when he says:

> The Sagas were written under terribly strong discipline. We modern people hardly have such discipline. Those writers never show their own feelings, but let the stories and characters speak entirely for themselves—objectively. It is an almost simpliste writing which is at the same time very sophisticated. Sometimes it leads you by the nose, and just when you feel it to be simpliste it surprises by its underlying complexity. The language is so rich, has been active in our literature for so many centuries. Our best poetry in pagan times, in the tenth century, in the Eddas, is a poetry you cannot hope to match now because that atmosphere, that quality of intellect, does not exist in our time.[2]

Laxness's own work, which earned him the Nobel Prize for literature in 1955, is a living refutation of such pessimism, and his admirers have even gone so far as to describe him as Iceland's first truly cosmopolitan writer since the Saga writers. One critic has cast him in the role of watchdog of cultural standards, seeing him as constantly urging Icelanders to examine their literature critically rather than to accept it unquestioningly in a glow of self-satisfaction, an attitude which could only lead to decay.

The key perhaps lies precisely in the mistaken emphasis on

uncritical emulation, the production of ever more faded carbon copies of the original, against which Laxness seems to be warning his readers, particularly the younger writers, who might see his diligent quarrying in the language's rich past as a mere process of copying the forms. In *Independent People*, for example, the readers' sympathies are enlisted for the innovatory poet in his conflicts with his imitative rival. In fact, what Laxness is doing is pointing out the essential modernity of classical Icelandic. 'They are young. I am old. So it is quite natural that they should read my books with some profit. Particularly they may find in the old language words which say modern things beautifully. When you reintroduce such words they are strikingly good.'[3] (Sometimes Laxness includes a translation in a European language, afterwards, to help the reader.)

Such quarrying is much easier in Icelandic than in any other European language. Where in English or any continental European language the disinterment of a phrase buried for 700 years might smack of archaism, if not literary necrophilia, in Icelandic it is merely a matter of taking an old friend from the bookshelf and dusting him off a little before use. Most reasonably educated Icelanders can read a classical text—indeed, an old German text, too—without great difficulty, recognising the majority of the words, although they may no longer have an every-day familiarity.

Icelandic, whose susurrations to the foreign ear seem akin to the high-speed action of a semi-silenced automatic vegetable scraper, has by the fortunes of history and geography survived in virtually the pristine form which the first settlers brought from their Norwegian home. The natural disasters in Iceland and the fortunes of Scandinavian politics in the fourteenth century, which cut off the island from all but the most tenuous contacts with the outside world, coincided with the onset of changes in the Germanic languages which have rendered the modern Scandinavian tongues incomprehensible to the Icelanders, and *vice versa*, despite their common origins. In classical times, no compunction was felt in absorbing words from other languages. In the impoverished times which followed such opportunity was small, but not unwelcome. In the last 150 years of Danish rule, however, resistance to the incursions of foreign words, particularly Danish ones, was seen as an act of necessary patriotism. Indeed, the movement for linguistic purity and for independence became complexly interwoven.

This attitude toward language has persisted to the present day. Thor Vilhjalmsson, president of the Icelandic Writers' Association, has described to me the anger and even accusations of treason which greeted the young generation of Icelandic poets a decade ago when they began, under European influence, to introduce revolutionary changes in style. He points out with nice irony that, while in medieval Europe thousands were going to the stake for heresy or witchcraft, such persecution was not customary in Iceland: the nearest Icelanders came to submitting their fellows to public immolation was when a poet had the temerity or misfortune to ignore the traditional rules of rhyme and alliteration. It marks a significant change in the development of the Icelandic cultural tradition that the work of contemporary younger poets is now both accepted and enjoyed by the majority of their fellow-countrymen.

Having an easily intelligible classical language, the 'purists' of the independence movement had no difficulty in coping with the modest demands of their primitive economy and social structure for new terms. Even after the dramatic changes in their material situation from 1940 onwards, linguistic 'purism' remained dominant, although not taken without a pinch of humour by such distinguished philologists as Professor Sigurdur Nordal who invented the word *tolva* ('number prophetess') for computer. Icelandic is practically unique in rejecting derivative terms for such words as telephone, taxi and television, which to the Icelander are *simi* ('the long thread'), *bifreid* ('moved waggon'), and *sjonvarp* ('view casting'). Occasionally the man on the other end of the telephone says 'oĸ', the children quip an Americanism from the latest television serial; but basically the linguistic bastions stand firm. Whether this is a permanent state of affairs, or even a healthy one, is another matter.

It is doubtful, indeed, whether linguistic purity can emerge completely unscathed from the demands of technical and scientific terminology in a complex and sophisticated society, but in Icelandic the inroads are unlikely to be disruptingly extensive. Such terms in the other languages of the Western world are generally derived from Greek or Latin roots, while the Asiatic and African languages borrow in turn from the European. Since Icelandic is rich in root words, there is no reason why modern scientific and technical terms cannot be fabricated from the old Icelandic itself, though it scarcely seems always worth the considerable effort involved. There remains the more important consideration that the ability of Iceland's all too small body of scientists and men trained in the modern professions to communicate with the main body of world knowledge, would be gravely impaired by too rigid a purism. Such communication is necessary not only so that they can learn about new developments but also gain the satisfaction of telling their scientific colleagues about their own advances, particularly in such fields as geology. Without such satisfactions, the already strong temptation for Icelandic doctors and scientists to emigrate may become irresistible.* One safeguard against such a situation is the fact that Icelanders are nearly all masters of at least English and sometimes several other languages. The tradition of being gifted with foreign tongues is an old one in Iceland. Not only did they enjoy mass literacy during the Commonwealth at a time of almost barbaric ignorance among the other peoples of Europe, but they had a higher proportion of Latin speakers than any other country.

* Many Icelandic doctors emigrate; there are said to be sixty working in Switzerland.

The purist movement is likely to receive a further stimulus from the decision of the Danish government to return to Reykjavík several hundred Icelandic manuscripts, now in the National Museum in Copenhagen. These are mainly examples of medieval literature. In Laxness's view, it is a literature rivalled in the Middle Ages only by the French.

It is doubtful, however, if any treasury of manuscripts can be of more than academic interest if the material when published does not stir an echo of recognition in the contemporary reader. Seen merely as some kind of missing link in an inviolable chain of petrifaction, the manuscripts can provide only a few years of pleasurable nostalgia to an ever-dwindling cultural gerontocracy. If they are to move the younger post-war generation, already perilously out of touch with its past, then they will have to be relevant in content. The religious writings are likely to have little appeal but the romances may perhaps beget an echo. Indeed, the manner of their reception may well help to solve the crucial question of whether the Icelanders are living on their past or in it.

☒

The principal stimulus to writers of all ages in Iceland is inevitably the country in which they live. This dramatic landscape is a setting against which only the best in literature or life can survive. It is the proper backcloth for giant trolls and magic, for heroes of more than human stature, such as are commemorated in the country's very place-names.

Into the strange convolutions of the lava one can read a thousand twisted faces; from the glacial heights only spirits can descend; and the basaltic clefts and volcanic jaws are a natural point of embarkation on a journey to the centre of the earth, as Jules Verne clearly realised. (In *Journey to the Centre of the Earth*, 1864, he sends the explorers down a volcanic crater to the north of Reykjavík.) The men who prevailed against, or even amidst, this 'heroic landscape' were heroes indeed, and the tales of their heroism, real or imaginary, quickly became the common property of a people whose own daily antagonists were these same elemental powers.

Against these powers the storyteller became a potent ally, almost a priest: his talismanic repetition of tales of demons and disasters, and of their conquest by courage and wit, was a weapon by which these perils could be averted in reality. Thus, in almost liturgical fashion, the oral tradition of storytelling took root; and, as priests have always been rewarded with the best of material things in exchange for their spiritual assistance, so the Icelandic storyteller was always a welcome guest, sure of an honoured seat and a good meal. Families had their own storytellers, and different artists worked their own peripheral embroideries of the central themes. But so great was the mobility of the population, not quite nomadic but often peripatetic, that on the back of the swift and nimble Icelandic pony was strapped the saddle of a common tongue carried from place to place. In Iceland there is, therefore, hardly any such thing as a regional or local dialect; all speak 'the poet's Icelandic'. Indeed, today it is argued that the purest Icelandic is still spoken by the least educated in the most remote parts, for their original speech has not been contaminated in any way by external post-war influences. It is often hard for the modern traveller to imagine that, behind the taciturn and silent face of the Icelander he meets somewhere in the wilds, there lurks a storyteller of wit and eloquence. But if he sits down patiently on a nearby stone digesting the silence, content to breathe in the atmosphere of so natural a backcloth for adventure as the Icelandic landscape, he will, in a few hours, be rewarded by his companion's breaking, unheralded, into steady narrative—perhaps even in English! Spellbound, the traveller can listen for hours till the storyteller, having done, leads him back to his house where he regales him with coffee and cakes and becomes as reserved as ever.

Living in a cross between a pastoral and an agricultural community, the Icelander, while he did not drive his flocks from place to place without permanent settlement, thought nothing of farming several different holdings for a few years at a time during his lifetime. At harvest time or in the fishing season, it was not unusual for a young man to hire out his labour to some distant farm and take his stories with him. In the twelfth and thirteenth centuries, the oral traditions in which such patterns of life were the common background were written down, principally in the Sagas, thus preserving the common language and the common culture which are the cornerstone of the Icelandic social structure.

For a foreigner to pin down the essence of these Sagas, he would need the rope which bound the wolf Fenrir, made of 'the roots of a mountain, the noise of a moving cat, the breath of a fish'. Without an Icelander's intimacy with the original language and thought, he cannot hope to make a fair judgement of the Sagas as literature. Yet when Icelanders attach so much importance to them, not just as literature but as part of the essence of their civilisation, some kind of objective assessment has to be attempted.

In many ways, the Sagas are highly topical literature. Although far from being historical novels, let alone histories, they are based on characters and events familiar to their readers and audiences. The complex genealogies, so meaningless and confusing to the casual foreign reader, were clear indices of character and status to those for whom they were intended: a combined parish register and family tree fraught with significance. Likewise taken for granted were the complex codes of honour, of etiquette and of hospitality whose observance or breach could be so significant; the role of fate; the allusions in the narrative to turbulent contemporary events. For the outsider reading them today, they can be understood only with the aid of a forest of footnotes. For the Icelander familiar, even today, with the genealogies and customs described, the Sagas still have a contemporary air.

159

Perhaps even more difficult for those whose own literary heritage has blossomed with the psychological novelist, the symbolist poet and the impressionist painter, is the style of the Sagas; and the better the translation the more strange the medium seems. The role of the reader of the Sagas is that of a privileged eye-witness of externals, for the authors make no subjective intrusions into the characters' thoughts and feelings. Is it a strength or a weakness that little subjective character-drawing is attempted? The narrative is all. The characters are allowed to speak for themselves, and the reader is invited to make of them what he will through their words and actions alone. This argues either a very sophisticated and imaginative audience, or a very simple one.

It would, of course, be misleading to think of Icelandic literature purely in terms of the Sagas with which it has largely come to be associated outside Iceland. There are enchanting folk tales which mirror the dream-world of an impoverished peasantry; the Rimur, epic narrative poems chanted in a special way, which followed the Sagas and used much of their subject matter; Dansar and Vikirakar, ballads to which people danced; the religious writing, prose and poetry of the eighteenth and nineteenth centuries; above all, perhaps, the scientific yet imaginative histories of which Ari in the *Landnámabók* and Snorri Sturlusson are the progenitors—all these are evidence of a perennial vigour and continuing manifestation of literary enthusiasm in many guises. But, as the Icelanders themselves put the Sagas at the centre of their literary and intellectual heritage, an outsider can only do the same.

A fairly typical Icelandic view of the Sagas is that of Guthmunder Finbogasson:

The Icelandic Sagas are justly famous for their great literary merits: their style, at once stately and homely, abounds in short pithy sentences; every thought is expressed, every event related in the most suitable language; the author's firm grip of things and his keen eye for the individuality of his characters are clearly revealed; there is in most of the Sagas a strong undercurrent of fate, sometimes faintly present even in the opening chapters where the descent of the persons is traced, and sometimes appearing in dreams, darkly foreshadowing the whole course of events; we are struck with the noble tranquillity of the author, his moderation and sober impartiality; always remaining behind the scene he lets his persons appear in words and deeds, as on a stage, each with his own particular mode of expression, his tricks of manner, his garb even. Nowhere is silence more eloquent, nowhere such vistas opened up between the lines as in the Icelandic Sagas. They show a mastery of the art of storytelling such as perhaps has never since been equalled in any literature until the nineteenth century.[4]

These are fairly extravagant claims, and even if one were to accept them without question they are claims which can be made with as much justification for a number of other eras of literary splendour in a wide variety of cultures. The wider influence of the Saga lies not in what was written or even in how skilfully it was written, but in the circumstances in which it was written and was read and preserved, and in its style. At a time when the great mass of writing in the rest of Europe was in Latin, the literature of Iceland was being created in the vernacular. While literary fashions in Europe were fostering a cult of highly artificial stylised writing, a kind of courtly code language, and were largely in verse-form, the authors of the Sagas were writing in prose with the realism, if not the obsessive subjectiveness, of the twentieth-century European novel.

The Sagas certainly have their own conventions and symbolism. The deaths of heroes and villains in combat are almost ritualistically stereotyped (the immolation at the climax of *Njáls Saga* is a striking exception, and some stereotype deaths are not without grim humour).*[5] But essentially the Sagas were a literature for all the people and reflected everyday experiences. While it is true that they had the advantage, as had other forms of Icelandic writing, of being created among a cultured and literate population which lacked any intellectually inferior or deprived class, they have in turn played a significant role (second only to that of Iceland's later almost universal poverty) in preventing the stratification of Icelandic society in later times.

Icelandic culture was essentially, indeed almost exclusively, a literary culture until the twentieth century. There was some music, but it was largely vocal rather than instrumental, an ornament or setting for the all-important word. Painting and sculpture require a far greater prosperity than, after the thirteenth century at least, was enjoyed in Iceland until modern times. Some of the wood carving which decorates the head boards of the bunks in the old *bathstofa*† are beautifully conceived and executed, but the visual arts went no further, until the paintings of Asgrimur Jonsson and the now internationally known Kjarval at the turn of this century and perhaps those of Sölvi Helgason in the last. This is scarcely surprising. But the strength and persistence of Iceland's literary culture was a cause of considerable astonishment and admiration to nineteenth-century outsiders discovering it for the first time. For example, one anonymous Englishman wrote:

> The contest of man with man gives place to the picture of man struggling with the elements—the tempest, the volcano, and the earthquake—for a miserable existence, and yet preserving among all the vicissitudes of his lot the advantages of civilisation, literature and religion. These facts give a

---

* As when Atli in *Grettirs Saga*, transfixed by a spear, comments as he expires: 'These broad-bladed spears are all the fashion nowadays.'

† The living room, but literally bath room, presumably from the habit of heating by throwing water on to the hot stones of the long fire to make steam.

moral interest to the history of Iceland, and invest it with a charm it would not otherwise possess. The most incurious cannot look with indifference on the spectacle of a people seemingly condemned by nature to spend their lives in laborious poverty and ignorance, becoming the poets and historians of the age, and creating a national literature amidst the perpetual snows and lava fields on this remote island.[6]

The reaction of such sympathetic observers was to think of the literature's being produced *despite* material poverty and a hostile environment, when in fact it was created *because* of these things. Icelandic literature was not only a defiance of the natural circumstances but to a large extent the only compensation for them. It was a compensation valued both because of the peculiar origins of a history which had created from the outset a literate and literary society embracing all its citizens, and also because the 'Golden Age' of literature reflected, in retrospect at least, a no less 'Golden Age' of prosperity.

Something of the spirit of these years of poverty is captured in the tale of an English traveller early in the nineteenth century who came to an isolated farm in the north, its low roof seeming to be on the point of collapse and the whole place reeking of misery and hunger. There in a corner, almost paralysed with cold, sat the poet-clergyman Jon Thorlaksson, translating Milton's *Paradise Lost* into Icelandic.

⊠

With such a dominantly literary tradition, the educational system itself has been inevitably an emphatically literary one until the last quarter of a century. Even now there is a heavy verbal and literary emphasis, with scientific and technical subjects still generally playing a secondary, if rapidly increasing, role. The major difference is that education is now more formalised and much less an integral part of family life than it was. As we saw in chapter 4, the role of the family and the community is still important in the rural areas; but, with the concentration of population in Reykjavík, the urban pattern of education sets the pace. The product of this pattern does not always meet with the approval of the older generation. Laxness has said of the young Icelanders that 'they are much worse educated than in olden times. They are more ignorant and have no discipline, so they tend to behave like geysers.'[7]

The truth of the matter is that the young are differently educated; they can no longer all concentrate on literacy at the expense of numeracy, when the materialistic society which their elders have created demands technical and scientific expertise rather than verbal facility. Certainly, the preoccupation with the less admirable aspects of their material society and the extent of hostility towards, or ignorance of, their traditional literature, are depressingly widespread. Whereas formerly it was a matter of prestige to know the Sagas, prestige is now rather a matter of having them. As one scholar rather sadly put it to me: 'Sagas by the metre are what count.'

Personally, I suspect that this is a phase through which the younger generation is passing. Literature and the era of poverty are so closely associated that a very understandable rejection of poverty in favour of the prosperity the young are determined to enjoy inevitably involves an initial rejection of the literature also. The very amenities of a modern advanced society have banished so much of that enforced leisure which was the seedbed of literary appreciation. However, a sharp awareness of the many erosive forces at work on Icelandic national identity may well drive the rebels back to their people's original source of spiritual strength.

It would be misleading, too, to suppose that this reaction to the old culture is universal. One can draw a portrait of a very different kind. Magnus Sigurdsson of Gilsbaki (near Reykholt, the home of Snorri Sturlusson), is in his early thirties and farms half of what was once his father's farm with three hundred ewes, nineteen cows and thirty-five hectares of arable land. It is hard work with long hours but, besides bringing him a good living, it leaves him 'a free man'. His home is comfortable, modern and well-furnished, and he built it himself with the aid of the local carpenter. The hospitality of his quiet wife is generous but unobtrusive. He is at first reluctant to talk about himself in the presence of strangers, but as the questions go on, courtesy demands they be answered and the answers themselves warm him to his theme: that the old and the new are not mutually exclusive but complementary. Though having had but little formal education, he can only be described as an intelligent and even a learned—or at last formidably knowledgeable—man. His primary schooling consisted of short spells in one or other of the farms in the district where the local children were gathered in for a few weeks in turn and visited and taught by an itinerant teacher. In all, his education probably didn't amount to twelve weeks in a year for four years or so. He went to a high school in Reykjavík for three winters but gave that up when he was twenty. Magnus has always been a voracious reader, everything from Agatha Christie to agricultural handbooks with a main diet of literature, history and world affairs. He takes an intense interest in what is happening in the world, and more particularly in what he calls 'the big flame' in Vietnam. Television has its place too: 'There's no use avoiding it.' On a recent radio contest (a kind of Icelandic 'Round Britain Quiz'), his erudition was astonishing. He took in his stride such questions as 'Who was the British representative at the peace negotiations after the Napoleonic Wars?'.

When Magnus was a boy, Iceland was, as he puts it, 'just as the early settlers found it'. He remembers the first car and the advent of the telephone when he was six. The changes since then have been enormous but he has adapted. His farming methods are modern and his use of capital investment schemes extensive, but the books on his wall are often old favourites. He likes to listen to the radio but also to read *Njáls Saga* to his children and encourage them to read it for themselves. He pays his labourers a good wage of 10,000 kronur a month for a skilled man, 5,000 for an unskilled, partly in cash and partly in ewes, for he recognises the difficulty a young man has today in raising enough money to invest in his own farm and live-stock when inflation is eating away at his savings. He gets on well with his neighbours: the learned pastor of Reykholt, Einar Guthnarsson, and the communist poet, Gudmundur Bodvarsson who is, of all things, translating Dante into Icelandic. His appreciation of the old social values of the community, however, has not led him to spurn the material prosperity of the new. Taxed with the suggestion that material prosperity might dilute the ancient spirit of his people, he simply replied: 'Prosperity gives a man a straight back.' Educated and reared in the old style, but brought up in and accepting the modern, Magnus has achieved that reconciliation between the two Icelands for which so many Icelanders hope.

Whether those brought up without any of the balancing influences of the past can fulfil these hopes is less certain. The walls of Reykjavík are often brightly bedaubed with the names of the Beatles or the Rolling Stones; and when one of the Stones was sentenced after a drug charge, it was front-page headline news in the Icelandic press—although one paper's headline read 'Beatle sent to clink'! These influences are exerted, not just through the usual channels of communication, but to a lesser extent through the small colonies of British beatniks and layabouts which in recent years have been attracted to Reykjavík by rumours that the streets are paved with gold.

It is certainly true that very high wages are to be had, but they have to be worked for, extremely hard, as they are by the young Scots and Englishmen who have earned themselves a good reputation on the trawlers. For the majority of the young-sters from abroad, the work involved comes as a shock and they soon give up any attempt to do any. They squat in overcrowded conditions in dockside warehouses or disused nissen huts, parasites on their host community. I visited one of these settlements, 'The Humpy Den', as the last remnants of its former inhabitants were departing. Dark but warm, crowded with bunks, littered with hundreds of empty bottles, and the walls daubed by brightly coloured drawings and sex slogans—some not without artistic merit—it was a real freebooters' den. There would, perhaps, be little enough harm in these communities except that in the past, since so few of them work, they have lived by stealing. Rival gangs of them in Reykjavík have engaged in stealing competitions to see who could take most in a single day. On one occasion, the 'eastsiders' beat the 'westsiders' by 11,000 kronur to 4,000. Between Christmas Day 1966 and June 30, 1967, twenty-seven British subjects were arrested on various charges in Reykjavík, principally larceny, malicious damage and assault. It is all too easy for Reykjavík youngsters, seeking new roots and influences, to assume these folk to be representative of the standards of the Western culture they strive to emulate.

Such emulation is the unavoidable consequence of Iceland's sudden transition from an isolated offshore island of the Arctic to a crossroads of modern communication. This is a change largely brought about by its strategic role in the North Atlantic radar defence ring and as a staging post for international transatlantic flights. This for the Icelanders has the advantage that stop-over visitors, and in particular distinguished musicians, can be snapped up for a single performance, as they are by the ever-watchful manager of the Reykjavík Radio Orchestra, before going on to their destination. The Icelanders have always been great travellers, but for long have been thwarted by economic circumstances. In recent years, they have taken avidly again to international travel as an early expression of their new prosperity.

The impact of the outside world has been not only direct but second-hand through television, radio and the press. Although there has been a radio service since 1934, an indigenous television service only came to Iceland in 1965. Some people in Reykjavík had, however, picked up the internal programme transmissions from the American base at Keflavík for several years. Indeed, it was these same transmissions which led many vehemently to oppose the introduction of a domestic service on the grounds that the influence of the American television transmissions was pernicious and any extension of the audience, by whomsoever served, would only be more so. Currently, the balance between indigenous and foreign material is about fifty-fifty, but the foreign material tends to be 'trashy' and it is hard to see how the children at least can avoid being conditioned by its speech idioms, albeit in a foreign tongue, and attitudes.

The radio service, which is entirely domestic in origin, is a much more intellectual medium in outlook. Fifty per cent of its output is music, 'pop', light and classical; and, although the rest of the transmission is talk and news material of a rather parochial nature, there is a daily international news bulletin and a weekly discussion–type programme usually encompassing foreign affairs.

The press, although primarily a vehicle for news and polemics, has its role to play in the nation's cultural life. In particular, it carries frequent examples of new work by local poets and critical dialogues in the form of readers' letters on subjects of literary and artistic importance.

Thus, the Icelandic public is in the strange position of being exceptionally well-informed in international political and economic affairs but of receiving, in the pop-star reporting and television soap opera, the very worst influences of Western cultural life. On the other hand, writers and artists are acutely aware of and exceptionally knowledgeable about the main European and American movements and achievements, and by comment, occasional imitation or influence transmit these cultural features at second-hand to their own public.

Outside influences are most clearly evident in the visual arts. Lacking any native tradition, Icelandic sculptors look to such figures as Moore and Hepworth, while the artists who are not being merely representational have followed the changing schools and fashions of European painters with keen if not uncritical interest. In Reykjavík itself, there is ample evidence on every hand. The variety of Icelandic domestic architecture is welcome relief from the drab uniformity of council-house grey or the poky bijoux-residences of some private developers in Britain, and offers yet further striking evidence of the Icelander's insistence on the expression of his individuality. Building techniques themselves—most houses are built of narrow concrete batons—are dictated by the need to provide for many different tastes rather than by economy.

But the most striking outdoor manifestation of Icelandic artistic individualism can be found in the house and garden of Asmundur Sveinsson on the east side of the city. I first saw his sculptures at that peculiarly Icelandic hour in summer when the sun gives a casual nod to the night, drops a curtsey below the horizon and is flaunting away again into the sky in new, dawn-stolen pastel shades that have suddenly displaced the flamboyance of a midnight evening. (Did that huge stone troll wink?; the sculpted bulk of "Woman's Power" stir contentedly in her sleep? Imagination! Or was it?)

If you are fortunate, as I was, to visit again in the prosaic light of mid-afternoon, you may come across a gnome asleep in the grass. He is dressed in baggy blue canvas trousers—surely a pair of jeans stolen from one of his precious giants—and huge broad braces designed, not to keep the trousers up but the owner down. Asmundur is the epitome of ebullience. A startled blink of tiny blue eyes pops at you like a champagne cork, and the effervescence bursts out in an uncontrollable cascade. He unlocks the semi-circular concrete studio he built himself—he likes his creations to breathe the fullness of space out of doors—and you know the movement in his works was not imagination.

Each sculpture comes alive in the presence of its creator: this miniaturised troll, this celestial clown who skips among so many props of iron and perspex, copper, wood and stone as if they were his living stage.

He loves the gigantesque, this small man; he sees it as an Icelandic quality, deriving inspiration from the mighty works of the ancient Egyptians. Humour, too, he must have and cannot abide those who would cloister art with sacerdotal whispers and Sunday suits, hide it in pompous seclusion. His "Eve", that apple breast held so satisfyingly in her hand, rousing the tooth-edge taste of every generation of man, strides from the garden of Eden in almost hilarious defiance. 'What? Evicted for a pesky apple, for finishing off the job of creation which you had left half-dead with perfection? You can keep your crepuscular garden!' Eve, insists Asmundur, must have been Icelandic.

Hell certainly is, or at least a neighbouring demonium with which Iceland has long enjoyed diplomatic relations and whose denizens she has tricked and artfully exploited again and again. Its flaming entrances and black windows erupt in every corner of the country, and some of its colours peer out of the canvases of Sverrir Haraldsson, who possesses a fluoroscopic vision of the bizarre and tortured landscape around him. He strips the countryside seen from his studio window down to its very fibres, depicting it in colours so vivid as to seem, to cold reason, almost ridiculous, impossible, but which are, in more essential reality, a perfect reflection of colours which must have passed, sub-conscious shadows only, across the mental retina of anyone who has travelled in Iceland. Now he is focusing this same vision on objects ever smaller, as though ultimately intending to paint the inside of the atom.

Sverrir had built himself a reputation as an abstractionist, in which style he worked until 1965, and some of these pictures can be seen in the Reykjavík National Gallery. Sadly, he has since been ignored by those responsible for buying for the gallery —was he held perhaps to have betrayed Iceland's sparse reputation for modernism?—and the public is thus deprived of some magnificent pictures. I was lucky enough to see some of them suspended against the backwall of his house in the garden where he took them out to show us—or rather, I suspect, to give himself an excuse to fly one of those intricate structures of coloured paper and balsawood which he began by making for his son and in which he now delights himself.

Most of these Icelandic artists and sculptors are little known outside Iceland, to the general public at least. Among artists, those already mentioned and such others as Svavar, Gudnasson, Skulasson and Trygvadottir, have some reputation, but less than they merit, and the man or gallery bringing them to Europe will deserve well of art-lovers. Painters in Iceland itself must also for a while resign themselves to having a less discriminating domestic public than writers, although this public is no less generous with its financial patronage. This is not surprising, for painting is a young art in Iceland, being less hardy than literature and rarely the child of total poverty, such as the country experienced until well into this century.

Already the average Icelander looks on original painting as essential furniture. In many houses, flats and farms, there is a mob of paintings jostling each other for space on walls which look like pages out of a postage-stamp album. Most of them are bad. But they are getting better, and more and more of them are in modern styles. It is likely, however, if you look at a picture on one of the crowded walls and then out of the window, that you will see the same scene. The Icelander likes his painting to be both familiar and representational; a local landscape is a very common anniversary or special birthday gift.

Yet there is, with the exception of one or two of the painters, surprisingly little imitation in any of the arts. The work of foreign writers, both in form and content, acts as a stimulus rather than as a pattern, and it is to their own leading creative artists, Laxness and the octogenerian painter Kjarval in particular, that the young Icelandic writers and artists look for inspiration and guidance. That these two men have been simultaneously able to blend the essentially Icelandic with an awareness and assimilation not only of modern art but of modern life as well is a most fortunate coincidence for Iceland. They epitomise what Professor Nordal has described as a national virtue.

> From the beginning of their history and on to the present day, the Icelanders have always welcomed innovation, been receptive of all kinds of foreign influence and quick to follow changes of fashion. But at the same time they have managed, gradually but always with essential success in the end, to keep control over these novelties and to adapt them to Icelandic traditions so that they have become, as it were, irrigating streams to refresh and make fertile, and not a destructive torrent doing irreparable harm to the native inheritance.[8]

But the most important foreign influence thus osmotically absorbed are not so much artistic as social. Thus Laxness emphatically denies the implication that Icelandic culture is decaying but admits that it is changing, precisely because Icelandic society has changed from a simple, rural, manual society to a predominantly complex, urban, mechanical one. When people are rapidly concentrated in large artificial communities, most of their cultural roots are inevitably torn up; and when material prosperity comes flooding in, aesthetic considerations are largely thrust aside in the scramble for the so-called 'good things' of life. In most nations with large or uniformly dense populations, total severance from the ancestral community and its ways seems inevitably to follow urbanisation, but Iceland has been partly (if only partly) saved from the consequences of urbanisation by the fact that there are so few Icelanders that the whole nation, however distributed, still remains a homogenous social unit, sufficiently limited in size for many cultural roots to retain their hold.

Admittedly, evidence of cultural activity is not at first apparent in the capital. The casual visitor to Rekjavík might not appreciate that he is in the capital of the most civilised nation in the world: a nation of a mere 195,000 people* which nevertheless supports more than 200 artists, sculptors, novelists, poets and playwrights; a nation which reads five times as many books per head as Britain.

Standing on a main street in the red light of a summer midnight watching the endlessly recirculating carloads of teenagers—some sober—you can feel little sense of the values of the classical literature of which the Icelanders are so proud. Can these youthful automaniacs, not even so unzombied as to be in pursuit of sex (who has to *pursue* it in Iceland?) be heirs to Gunnar and Gisli, daughters of Unn and Bergthora?

Perhaps more truly so than the first condemnatory glance of a visiting stranger might assume. The very purposelessness with which they pervehiculate the town, girls in this, boys in that opulent importation of tin-can cultures, shows that perhaps they find the mid-Atlanticism as tasteless as the huge bananas of the Hveragerthi geyser hothouses with their *papier-mâché* flavour. Laxness reacts with a touch of anger to the fact that many of these young people neither know nor care about their literature: anger, not at them in their innocence, but at that 'overheated, neurotic, alcoholic, erotomaniacal literature' on which they have been brought up.

Unfortunately, the frenetic modernity of Reykjavík may be the only impression which the lightning tourist, blinded by the Leica in his eye, will ever get. But if he stays a while, he will realise that 'culture' is not overtly in evidence precisely because culture pervades every aspect of Icelandic life.

In Britain, if you declare a colleague at work to be a poet, or, worse, blushingly lay claim to such a failing yourself, your hearer may eye you askance. In Iceland, such a statement is

* There are more people alive today in the city of Glasgow than there have been Icelanders in the whole history of the island.

made with the perfunctory lack of self-consciousness with which one might express a preference for tweed or for coffee. Even the last sitting of each session of the Althing is conducted entirely in verse.* Indeed, the wonder would be if a man were *not* a poet, unless of course he wrote prose or sculpted or painted pictures. The Icelanders' attitude to such cerebral amputation as we regard as normal was described by Thor Vilhjalmasson:

> I hope it can still be said that everyone who cannot make a neat couplet or a nice rhyme is to be considered some kind of idiot. You may worry that something has happened to him: he may have been hit on the head by a stone or struck by a flower pot when walking in some foreign city so that the poor fellow cannot make poetry any more.[9]

In Iceland, a man should as soon be able to turn a verse as a lathe. Both kinds of activity are considered essential to his well-being as a man, and therefore both are useful arts. If one had to go it would be the lathe. This sense of values is evident from the position of writers and artists in society. It is shown not just in high status, although they enjoy that, but by the fact that it is possible for so many of them to make a living entirely or primarily from their art. The unquestioned acceptance of their role in society receives formal acknowledgement in the small stipends which the state pays to most authors, painters and sculptors. Although the manner of their allocation and distribution among those concerned is a subject of dispute, it does at least show an official recognition of the importance of the creative artist, and particularly the writer.

But the creative artist's standing and 'viability' are not due to state patronage. What really sustains him is the patronage of the public. In the case of writers, this is a highly discriminating and widely read, if entrenchedly conservative, public. Many fancy their own powers as creators, all as critics. New trends

* To most people, this is its most fruitful session and the members often devote much time and energy to composing their speeches for the occasion.

have a hard struggle to take root. But Laxness, once looked on as a radical, is now the darling of the establishment; and if Vilhjalmsson, with his impressionistic, subjective, prose and 'fish-eye' view of life, so alien to the objectivity of the Sagas, and the younger nonconformist poets, had difficulty in gaining acceptance for some years, they have now won their battle and their public. The fact remains that a new volume of poetry will sell as many copies among the Icelanders as it would among two hundred times as many Englishmen.

Such sensitivity of reaction in a discriminating public gives satisfaction enough to the Icelandic writer. Feeling that the language is an instrument capable of yielding an infinite variety and richness of expression, he does not hanker for the wider audience he might gain by using some other tongue. Laxness's confession that 'it has been my great joy in life to write in this tremendously interesting language which has a unique past' is echoed by every Icelandic writer. This is true even of those who, like Vilhjalmsson, for example, have revolutionised the old traditions in style and content. In the early part of the century, many young Icelandic writers went to Denmark, wrote in Danish, and in some cases, such as that of Gunnar Gunnarsson, made considerable reputations. The majority returned, as if compelled, to Iceland. Laxness himself, although later to become an inveterate traveller, decided to remain in Iceland at the time of the exodus and always to keep it as his firmly rooted base. That so little Icelandic writing is translated into English is our loss rather than the Icelanders'. Only seven of Laxness's inimitable novels, two of Vilhjalmsson's books and relatively few other modern works are available in English.

The critical question is the extent to which the ordinary citizen remains involved in all these cultural activities. They have been formalised, almost institutionalised, in the profusion —at least in *per capita* terms—of theatres, libraries, art galleries and so on. But who are the new patrons of these institutions?

Has the provision of focal points for cultural activity as something to which one 'goes out', withdrawn culture from the domestic surroundings of which it was such an integral part? Nordal's verdict on the fate of the old Rimur, for example, is unequivocal:

> ... we must face the facts as they are. Rimur will never again be sung as part of an evening's entertainment in the farmhouses.* For one thing, there are now so few people on the farms that *kvoldvokur* ['sing-song'†] in the old style are almost out of the question, and if they listen to anything, they listen to the wireless. Young people do not read Rimur and much would be incomprehensible to them if they did. In the past it could be said that there were always some Rimur available on every farm, books always in a worse tattered state than any others. Now what is left of them is collected by a few bookworms, the pages are washed and bound, they are locked up in cupboards and preserved as specimens of a bygone age, like hornspoons, bedboards, and whale oil lamps.[10]

Even in such an out-of-the-way place as Isafjord (where Laxness once spoke about poetry to an audience of 120, over half of whom were themselves active poets), the preference, when the choice is available, among the young at least, seems to be for a good cinema show, pop group or dance rather than for older, more consciously literary forms of entertainment. The editor of the local paper expressed the view that in another twenty years all the old roots will have disappeared.

Already there is little reading of the Sagas or of classical poetry. These are now regarded as something to be set for a school task rather than to be read for pleasure. As elsewhere

---

* They are sometimes presented on the radio, and Rimur preservation societies also exist.

† *Kvoldvokur* is more literally translatable as 'evening watch' or 'evening wake'—though without the funeral connotation of the latter!

in Europe, thrillers and romances are the more popular entertainment reading, and their heroes the models and dream-
images of the young. The Saga hero has ceased to be a common
daily exemplar, replaced by The Saint or Barbarella, and it is
less and less likely that a man confronted with a difficult
practical problem might say, unselfconsciously, to himself, 'It
would have been nothing to Skarp Hedin. How would he set
about it?' as if the Saga hero were a neighbouring farmer still
alive.

                                   ☙

It would, however, be short-sighted to suppose that the presence
of so much that is worst in Western society, from comics to the
rash of Coke bottles which litter even the most secluded beauty
spot, implies its unhesitating acceptance by the Icelanders.

One of the most remarkable things about the Icelandic people
is their tolerance: a tolerance which sometimes verges exasperat-
ingly on indolence and indifference. In some ways it is eminently civilized, as in their attitude to extramarital sexual
relations and the illegimate child and its mother. The illegitimate birth rate is a staggering 28·3 per cent. In fact, this is
due partly to the long-accepted custom of a man's having a
'housekeeper' and avoiding the expense of marrying her, and
partly to the present-day tax advantages to be gained by the
couple who live together and raise a family without getting
married. But the chief explanation for this figure is that no one
can be bothered to make a major moral issue of illegitimacy,
any more than they can of drunkenness and other forms of
behaviour regarded as criminal, or at least anti-social, elsewhere. Even suicide is looked on as a strictly personal matter,
and where everyone knows everyone else verdicts of suicide
are rarely brought in, even in clear cases, lest relatives be up-
set. In fact it was rumoured with some authority that, in one
month (February) far into the depressing long winter of 1967,
more than twenty people committed suicide, and those

concerned with sociological problems (there are no professional sociologists in Iceland) were worried at what they felt to be a growing trend in their materialist society. On the other hand, that society as a whole was deeply shocked when in 1967 a lawyer murdered his wife, for murder is so rare—intolerance just isn't taken to that extreme—that there have been only six cases in the past thirty years.

Icelandic tolerance may have an element of laziness in it, but it is far more an inbred result of the growing recognition over the centuries that in a hostile environment there must be strict priorities of enmity and that one's fellow man comes well down the list. Tolerance is also the product of Icelandic history. Since the end of the thirteenth century, there have been no internal wars. Nor, and more important, has Iceland been involved in the endless international conflicts which have afflicted the rest of the world. It is arguable that intolerance and hatred are socially generated phenomena, that without any collective objects of hatred the individuals of any group will probably lose their residual personal capacity for hatred. If the group is sufficiently large or overcrowded, then hatred may find an outlet within, through factionalism and personal animosities. But, in Iceland, the number of potential enemies is so small that the identity of interest between a person and any such potential enemy nearly always precludes the practical expression of hatred. Your neighbour on the next farm or in the next boat is so often an essential ally against the hostile elements, so often a man or woman on whose support you rely for your own preservation and survival, that there is no room for enmity. The enemies of the Icelander are inanimate objects, although they may seem to border on the animate in their multiple manifestations of apparent hostility. Where man is concerned, the Icelanders seem to have lost the habit of hate.

This attitude of mind is not merely a negative one, resulting from the absence of opportunities for hatred. Because there are so few Icelanders, because they have so much living space, though also an unusual mobility, they are not, as so many of us are, overwhelmed by the multitudinousness of mankind. They can feel that they know most of the members of their community and could know them all if they wished. This minister is a cousin of my brother-in-law, that one is a friend of my mother's, this famous artist goes riding with me, I drink coffee with that great writer twice a week, and so on. Everyone, in fact, is a neighbour. You always call any man or woman by his or her first name, be it a trawler-hand addressing the prime minister or *vice versa*, as if he were a member of the family— as in a sense he is. Even the telephone directory is listed under first names not surnames.

The fact that, in the first half of this century, the population has increased two and a half times above the high point of the Commonwealth, with Reykjavík alone containing more people than the whole island in those days, is one of the most insidious threats to the Icelandic character. It has not yet reached critical mass; 200,000 Icelanders is a notion that can still be comfortably encompassed by the ordinary citizen. But the half million which may be deduced from an extrapolation of the present trends to the next century would be a different matter.

Nowhere is the present sense of a national family more effectively shown than in the prominence given to funeral services and obituaries, not only in the press but on the radio. Where else in the world would you find two hours of broadcasting every day devoted to different funeral services throughout the country, and the largest revenue item from radio advertising coming from paid obituary notices? In such a society, a sense of alienation is rare; everyone feels he belongs, that he is somebody. It is this that makes Iceland such an eminently sane country, and one of the ingredients which make it also highly civilised. The other is the organic nature of its culture.

It is not just a matter of unconscious cultural standards, although again and again you are brought back to the recognition that art and literature in Iceland are an integral part of daily life, not an occasional activity. It is the manner in which this culture exists which makes the Icelanders such an essentially civilised people. Throughout the rest of the world there seems to be developing a far more dangerous division than that which Lord Snow sees as opening between the 'two cultures': the division between words and action, the universal prevalence in politics, science, the arts, of multiple-think and newspeak. This must be potentially disastrous for a social structure which has evolved on the assumption that there is at least some tenuous connection between words and action. In Iceland, this divorce does not exist—with rare exceptions. The Icelandic society of the early settlement was one in which a man won his rewards by seizure and courage in battle, or through gifts bestowed for his poetic skill and the charms of his tongue. As often as not, the same man would win wealth, and the all-important honour, in both ways. There was no conflict between art and action, and sometimes it became impossible to draw a dividing line between them. This balance between the merits of words and action persisted after the warrior and chieftain had become but farmer and fisherman; they were all nevertheless poets. It is this unity, and its expression in a free, cultured and tolerant society, which makes Iceland the world's last truly civilised nation. Its institutions could change or collapse, its economy crash, yet it would remain essentially the same. The gravest threat to its civilisation comes from the prospect of limitless prosperity and its consequent social and demographic disruptions. Adversity, natural and man-made, the Icelanders have not only survived but transmuted over the centuries. It would be a tragedy reaching far beyond their own rocky shores if they were unable to survive good fortune.

Appendix I

The Constitution of the
Republic of Iceland (1944)

CHAPTER ONE

ARTICLE I

Iceland is a republic with a constitutional government.

ARTICLE 2

The legislative power is jointly vested in the Althing (Parliament) and the President of the Republic of Iceland. The Executive power is exercised by the President and other governmental authorities in accordance with this Constitution and other laws of the land. The judicial power is exercised by the judiciary.

CHAPTER TWO [*The President and the Executive*]

ARTICLE 3

The President shall be elected by the people.

ARTICLE 4

Any person not less than thirty-five years of age who fulfils the qualifications necessary to vote for the Althing, with the exception of the residence qualification, is eligible for the Presidency.

ARTICLE 5

The President shall be elected by a direct, secret ballot of those who are entitled to vote for the Althing. A presidential candidate shall be formally proposed by not less than fifteen hundred voters and not more than three thousand. The candidate, if there is more than one, who receives the majority of votes, is the legally elected President. If there is only one candidate he is returned unopposed.

Further provisions shall be made by law for the candidature and election of the President, and it may be provided thereby that the number of proposers shall in each quarter of the country be proportionate to the number of voters.

ARTICLE 6

The President's term of office begins on the first day of August and ends on the thirty-first day of July four years later. The election of the President takes place in June or July of the year in which the term ends.

ARTICLE 7

If the President dies or resigns prior to the expiry of his term, a new President shall be elected for a period ending on the thirty-first day of July of the fourth year from the election.

ARTICLE 8

If the office of President becomes vacant or if the President temporarily cannot hold office because of residence abroad, illness or other reasons, the Prime Minister, the Speaker of the United Althing, and the Chief Justice of the Supreme Court shall exercise the presidential power. The Speaker of the United Althing shall preside at their meetings. In a divergence of opinion the majority shall prevail.

ARTICLE 9

The President must not be a member of the Althing or receive emoluments in the interest of any public or private enterprise.

Allowances from the national treasury to the President or those who execute the presidential authority shall be established by law. It shall be unlawful to reduce presidential allowances during the term of office.

ARTICLE 10

On assuming office the President takes an oath or makes an affirmation to uphold the Constitution. Two identical texts shall be made, one to be preserved by the Althing and the second to be enrolled in the National Archives.

ARTICLE 11

The President is not answerable for his official actions. The same applies to those who execute the presidential authority.

The President cannot be prosecuted on a criminal charge except with the consent of the Althing.

The President shall cease to hold office before his term expires if this is approved by a plebiscite held in accordance with a resolution adopted by three-fourths of the members of the United Althing. This plebiscite shall be held within two calendar months from the date of adoption of the said resolution, during which period the President shall not hold office.

If the said resolution be defeated in the plebiscite, the Althing shall be immediately dissolved and preparations made for a new election.

ARTICLE 12

The President shall have his residence in Reykjavík or the environs.

ARTICLE 13

The President exercises his authority through his Ministers. The Cabinet has its seat in Reykjavík.

ARTICLE 14

The Cabinet is responsible for all acts of the Government. The responsibility of Ministers is established by law. The Althing may impeach Ministers for the discharge of their official duties. The Court of Impeachment has jurisdiction in such matters.

ARTICLE 15

The President appoints the Cabinet and accepts ministerial resignations. He determines the number of Ministers and assigns their duties.

ARTICLE 16

The President presides over the State Council which is composed of his Ministers.

Laws and important Government measures shall be submitted to the President in Council.

ARTICLE 17

Cabinet meetings shall be held in order to discuss new legislative proposals and important political measures. Furthermore, Cabinet meetings shall be held when one of the Ministers so desires. The Prime Minister shall preside over such Cabinet meetings.

ARTICLE 18

The Minister who has proposed a measure shall, as a rule, submit it to the President.

ARTICLE 19

The Presidential signature countersigned by a Minister validates a legislative measure or an act of Government.

ARTICLE 20

The President shall make the appointments to all such offices as are provided by law.

No person may hold office unless he is an Icelandic citizen. Each official shall take an oath or make an affirmation to uphold the Constitution.

The President may remove from office any official whom he has appointed.

The President may transfer officials from one office to another on the condition that their official income shall not be diminished, and that they shall have an option between such transfer and retirement with a pension or old-age allowance as prescribed by law.

Certain classes of officials in addition to those mentioned in Art. 61 may be legally exempted.

ARTICLE 21

The President concludes treaties with other states. Except with the consent of the Althing, he may not make such agreements if they entail renouncement of or servitude on territory or territorial waters or if they imply constitutional changes.

ARTICLE 22

The President shall summon the Althing every year and determine when the session shall close. The Althing must not adjourn till the Budget has been passed. The President may also summon the Althing to extraordinary sessions when necessary.

ARTICLE 23

The President may adjourn meetings of the Althing for a certain period of time, but not for more than two weeks nor more than once a year. But the Althing may authorise the President to deviate from these provisions.

ARTICLE 24

The President may dissolve the Althing. A new election must take place before two calendar months have elapsed from the date of dissolution. The Althing shall reassemble not later than eight calendar months after its dissolution.

ARTICLE 25

The President may have Bills and proposals for resolutions submitted to the Althing.

ARTICLE 26

If the Althing has passed a Bill it shall be submitted to the President for approval not later than two weeks after it has been passed, and upon such approval shall be enforced as law. If the President disapproves a Bill it shall nevertheless become valid but shall as soon as circumstances permit be submitted to a plebiscite by secret ballot and if rejected shall become invalid but otherwise retain its legal force.

ARTICLE 27

All laws shall be published. The form of publication and the enforcement of laws shall be in accordance with the law of the land.

ARTICLE 28

In the event of extreme urgency the President may issue provisional laws in the interval between sessions of the Althing. Such laws must not, however, be contrary to the Constitution and they shall always be submitted to the Althing as soon as it reassembles.

If the Althing does not approve a provisional law it shall become invalid.

A Provisional Budget may not be issued if the Althing has passed the Budget for the fiscal year.

ARTICLE 29

The President may decide that the prosecution for an offence be withdrawn if there are cogent reasons. He grants pardon and amnesty. Except with the consent of the Althing he may not absolve a Minister from prosecution or from the sentence imposed by the Court of Impeachment.

ARTICLE 30

The President grants, either in person or through the Government, exemptions from laws in accordance with the prevailing practice.

CHAPTER THREE [*The Althing: Composition*]

ARTICLE 31

The Althing shall be composed of up to 60* members elected by the people in a secret ballot. There shall be:

* Amended from 52 in 1950.

Appendix I: The Constitution of the Republic of Iceland

(*a*) Eight members for Reykjavík. Their election shall be by proportional representation. An equal number of substitutes shall be elected at the same time and in the same manner.*

(*b*) Six members, one for each of the following towns: Hafnarfjördur, Isafjördur, Siglufjördur, Akureyri, Seydisfjördur and Vestmannaeyjar.*

(*c*) Twenty-seven members for the constituencies, other than towns, which are at present represented by one or two members. In two-member constituencies election shall be by proportional representation and an equal number of substitutes shall be elected at the same time and in the same manner. If a member for any of the constituencies, which are represented by one member only, dies during his term of election, another member shall be elected in his place for the remainder of the period.*

(*d*) Up to eleven members for equalisation between parties, so that each of them shall be represented as nearly as possible in proportion to the number of votes obtained in the General Election. At the General Election any party may present a nation-wide panel of candidates, in which case voters are free to vote either for such a panel or for the candidate or candidates of the electoral district. Candidates of a party which has presented a nation-wide panel at a General Election and obtained equalisation seats shall at the conclusion of the election occupy these in the order which they take on the panel. At least every other of the ten topmost seats of such a panel shall be occupied by candidates of constituencies outside Reykjavík. The equalisation seats shall in other respects by arranged in accordance with the Election Act. An equal number of substitutes shall be elected for equalisation seats at the same time and in the same manner.

The members shall be elected for a period of four years.

ARTICLE 32

The Althing is divided into an Upper and a Lower House.

* Sections (*a*), (*b*) and (*c*) are subsequently amended; see page 186.

187

One-third of the members sit in the Upper House, and two-thirds in the Lower House. Should the number of members be such as to make impossible a division by thirds the odd members shall sit in the Lower House.

ARTICLE 33

All persons, men and women, who are 20* years of age or older at the time of election, are Icelandic subjects and have been domiciled in the country for five years prior to an election, shall have the right to vote. No person shall have the right to vote unless of unblemished character and financially responsible.

A married woman shall be considered financially responsible even though her property be held in the name of her husband.

Further enactments regarding parliamentary elections are laid down in the Election Act.

ARTICLE 34

Every citizen qualified to vote is eligible for the Althing.

Judges who do not hold administrative office are not eligible for the Althing.

CHAPTER FOUR [*The Althing: Powers and Procedure*]

ARTICLE 35

The Althing shall be summoned for a regular session every year on the fifteenth day of February or, if a holiday, on the following weekday, unless the President has already appointed another date earlier in the year for the opening of the session.

This may be amended by law.

ARTICLE 36

The Althing is inviolate. No person may disturb its peace or violate its freedom.

ARTICLE 37

The Althing shall be convened in Reykjavík but under special

* Amended from 21 in 1966.

circumstances the President may convene the Althing at some other place in Iceland.

ARTICLE 38

Each House is individually entitled to introduce and pass Bills and proposals for resolutions. Each House individually or unitedly may send addresses to the President.

ARTICLE 39

Each House may appoint committees of its members in order to investigate important matters of public interest. The House may grant authority to such committees to demand reports, oral or written, from Government officials or private persons.

ARTICLE 40

No tax may be imposed, altered or abolished except by law; nor may loans binding upon the State be raised, nor any State property or interest therein be sold or in any other way disposed of except by law.

ARTICLE 41

No disbursements may be made unless authorised in the Budget or the Supplementary Budget.

ARTICLE 42

A Finance Bill for the coming fiscal year containing an estimate of the revenue and expenditure of the State shall be submitted to the Althing immediately on reassembling for a regular session.

Finance Bills and Supplementary Finance Bills shall be introduced in the United Althing and passed in three readings.

ARTICLE 43

The United Althing shall elect by proportional representation three salaried Auditors, who shall annually audit the national revenue and expenditure accounts to ascertain whether the entire revenue has been included and whether any unauthorised disbursements have been made. They may, individually or jointly, request all reports and documents which they may deem necessary. The accounts for each fiscal year shall then be incorporated into one aggregate account and a Bill for the approval thereof be submitted to the Althing together with the comments of the Auditors.

The Auditors are, individually or jointly, entitled to examine the accounts and books of the State Treasurer as well as those of the Ministries for the current or past year. They shall submit their comments, if any, to their successors in writing.

ARTICLE 44

No Bill, with the exception of the Finance and the Supplementary Finance Bill, may be passed without three readings in each House.

ARTICLE 45

The first House which passes a Bill shall submit the Bill in the form in which it was passed to the other House. Should amendments be made here the Bill shall be returned to its source of origin, where, if again amended, the same procedure shall be followed.

Should no agreement be reached both Houses shall meet in a conclave, and the matter be settled in one reading by the United Althing.

When the Althing meets in a joint session more than one half of the members of each House must be present and take part in the voting in order to constitute a quorum, the majority of votes prevailing in all particulars. Bills, other than Finance and Supplementary Finance Bills, shall not be finally passed unless supported by two thirds of the votes cast.

ARTICLE 46

The Althing itself decides whether its members are legally elected and also whether a member is disqualified.

ARTICLE 47

Each new member shall as soon as his election has been approved take an oath or make an affirmation to uphold the Constitution.

ARTICLE 48

Members of the Althing are bound solely by their conviction and not by any orders from their constituents.

Government officials who may be elected to the Althing do not require the permission of the Government to accept election, but they must take measures for the discharge of their functions in a manner deemed satisfactory by the Government and without expense to the Treasury.

ARTICLE 49

No member may be arrested for debt during a session of the Althing without the permission of the House of which he is a member, nor may he be placed under restraint or an action brought against him unless he is found *in flagrante delicto*.

No member may be made responsible outside the Althing for statements made by him in the Althing, except with the permission of the House concerned.

ARTICLE 50

If a member is disqualified he shall forfeit his seat.

ARTICLE 51

Ministers by virtue of their office have the right to attend meetings of the Althing and are entitled to take part in the debates as often as they may desire, subject to parliamentary procedure; but they have a right to vote only if they are at the same time elected members of the Althing.

ARTICLE 52

Each House and the United Althing elects its own Speaker.

ARTICLE 53

Neither House may pass a resolution unless more than one half of the members of the House are present at the meeting and register their votes.

ARTICLE 54

Each member is at liberty to introduce in the House of which he is a member any matter of general nature and to request a Ministerial report thereon, subject to the permission of that House.

ARTICLE 55

Neither House may admit any matter unless introduced by a member of that House.

ARTICLE 56

If a House does not find any reason to pass a resolution it may refer the subject to a Minister.

ARTICLE 57

The meetings of both Houses and those of the United Althing shall be public. But the Speaker or the quorum stipulated by the rules of the House may demand that all non-members be excluded. The meeting shall then decide whether the matter shall be debated at a public or a closed session.

ARTICLE 58

The rules of procedure of the United Althing and those of both Houses shall be determined by law.

CHAPTER FIVE [*The Judiciary*]

ARTICLE 59

The organisation of the judiciary cannot be established except by law.

ARTICLE 60

The judges shall settle all disputes as to the extent of the power of administrative officers. But no one seeking a judicial ruling thereunto can evade obeying temporarily an order of the administrative officers by submitting the matter to judicial decision.

ARTICLE 61

Judges shall in the performance of their official functions be guided solely by the law. Judges who do not also hold administrative offices cannot be discharged from office except by a judicial ruling, nor may they be transferred to another office against their will except in the event of reorganisation of the judiciary. A judge who has reached the age of 65 may, however, be allowed to resign from office without reduction of salary.

CHAPTER SIX [*The Church*]

ARTICLE 62

The Evangelical-Lutheran Church shall be the State Church and as such it shall be supported and protected by the State.

This may be altered by law.

ARTICLE 63

The people are entitled to form societies for the worship of God in conformity with their individual convictions; but nothing may be preached or practiced which is prejudicial to public order and morality.

ARTICLE 64

No person may lose his civil or national rights on account of his religious conviction nor must he therefore refuse to perform any civic duty.

No person is obliged to contribute to any religious worship against his conviction.

If a person is not a member of the State Church of Iceland nor of any other recognised religion he shall pay to the University of Iceland or to a designated scholarship fund of that University dues otherwise payable to the Church.

This may be amended by law.

CHAPTER SEVEN [*Civil and Social Rights; Taxation; Constitutional Amendment*]

ARTICLE 65

Any person who is arrested shall be brought before a judge without undue delay, and if not released at once, the judge shall, within 24 hours, give a reasoned ruling as to whether he shall be detained. If the person may be released on bail the ruling shall contain provisions as to its nature and amount.

An appeal to a higher court may immediately be made against a judicial ruling, the procedure of notification and appeal against such rulings being the same as in criminal cases.

No person may be taken into custody for an offence merely punishable by fines or imprisonment.

ARTICLE 66

The home shall be inviolate. Houses may not be searched, nor any letters or other documents be detained and examined, except by judicial warrant or by a special provision of law.

ARTICLE 67

The right of private ownership is inviolate. No one shall be forced to surrender his property unless required by public exigency, in which case a law must be passed and full compensation paid.

ARTICLE 68

No alien may acquire citizenship except by law. The right of aliens to own immovable property shall be subject to law.

ARTICLE 69

No restriction may be imposed upon individual freedom of employment, unless legislated for as being required by the common good.

ARTICLE 70

Whosoever is unable to provide for himself or his dependants shall, subject to duties prescribed by law, be entitled to support from public funds, unless his maintenance rests upon others.

ARTICLE 71

If parents cannot afford to educate their children, or if the children are orphaned or destitute, their education and maintenance must be defrayed from public funds.

ARTICLE 72

Every person has the right to express his thoughts in print, but is responsible for such utterances before the courts. Censorship and other restrictions on the freedom of the press may never be enacted.

ARTICLE 73

Societies may be formed for every lawful purpose without previous authorisation. No society may be dissolved by act of Government, but it may be temporarily suspended, in which case an action for dissolution must immediately be brought.

ARTICLE 74

People are entitled to assemble unarmed. The police have the right to be present at all public gatherings. Open-air meetings may be forbidden when it is feared that they may cause riots.

ARTICLE 75

Every person able to carry arms shall be obliged to take part in the defence of the country according to provisions which may be detailed by law.

ARTICLE 76

The right of autonomy of urban and rural communities under the supervision of the Government shall be determined by legislation.

ARTICLE 77

Taxation shall be determined by legislation.

ARTICLE 78

Privileges reserved for nobility, titles and rank must never be enacted.

ARTICLE 79

Proposals, whether amendatory or supplementary to this Constitution, may be introduced at regular as well as extraordinary sessions of the Althing. If the proposal is passed by both Houses, the Althing shall be dissolved immediately and a General Election be held. If both Houses pass the resolution without amendments it shall be ratified by the President of the Republic and come into force as a Constitutional Act.

If the Althing passes an amendment to the status of the Church affairs, according to Article 62, it shall be submitted to a plebiscite by secret ballot for acceptance or rejection.

ARTICLE 80

By this Constitutional Act the Constitution of the Kingdom of Iceland, of the eighteenth day of May nineteen hundred and twenty, the Constitutional Acts of the twenty-fourth of March nineteen hundred and thirty-four, of the first day of September nineteen hundred and forty-two and the fifteenth day of December nineteen hundred and forty-two shall cease to be in effect and become null and void.

ARTICLE 81

This Constitutional Act comes into force when the Althing so resolves, provided that the Act has been passed in a secret ballot by the majority of voters in the country.

TEMPORARY PROVISIONS

Upon the coming into force of this Constitution the United Althing shall elect the President of Iceland for the first time in accordance with the provisions governing the election of the Speaker of the United Althing. The Presidential term of office

Appendix I: The Constitution of the Republic of Iceland

shall expire on the thirty-first day of July nineteen hundred and forty-five.

Aliens who, prior to the coming into effect of this Constitution, have been enfranchised and made eligible for the Althing or have obtained the right to hold public office shall retain the said rights. Danish citizens who under Article 75 of the Constitution of the eighteenth day of May nineteen hundred and twenty would have obtained such rights shall, from the coming into force of this Constitutional Act until six calendar months after negotiations regarding the rights of Danish citizens in Iceland can be commenced, also acquire and retain the said rights.

RESOLUTION

Resolution concerning the coming into force of the Constitution of the Republic of Iceland (*Passed by the Althing on the sixteenth day of June nineteen hundred and forty-four*)

WHEREAS the provisions of Article 81 of the Constitution of the Republic of Iceland as to ballot by all voters of the country have been fulfilled,

THE ALTHING with reference to the said Article

RESOLVES THAT the Constitution shall come into force upon Saturday the seventeenth day of June nineteen hundred and forty-four with a declaration by the Speaker of the United Althing in session.

In accordance with a declaration by the Speaker of the United Althing, convened at Lögberg on Thingvellir on the seventeenth day of June nineteen hundred and forty-four the Constitution came into force at two o'clock in the afternoon of that same day.

Appendix II

Statistical Tables

TABLE I

Vessel-types and tonnage of Iceland's fishing fleet, 1905–67

Year	Decked Sailing Vessels		Steam-powered Long-liners		Deep-sea Trawlers		Decked Motor Vessels over 12 tons		Totals	
	No.	Gr. regd t.	No.	Gr. regd t.	No.	Gr. regd t.	No.	Gr. regd t.	No.	Gr. regd t.
1905	166	7,938	2	163	1	151	—	—	169	8,252
1910	139	6,241	2	199	6	1,106	1	20	143	7,506
1920	39	1,190	2	223	28	8,730	120	3,538	189	13,681
1930	—	—	40	4,335	42	13,993	224	5,506	306	24,061
1939	—	—	25	2,891	37	12,855	310	8,684	372	24,430
1945	—	—	14	2,832	28	9,383	385	14,315	427	26,530
1955	—	—	—	—	44	28,476	481	24,314	525	52,790
1963	—	—	—	—	43	30,754	610	39,872	654	70,626
1965	—	—	—	—	38	26,708	601	49,550	639	76,258
1967	—	—	—	—	30	21,491	574	59,471	604	80,962

Notes

1. In 1876, there were 3,208 open rowing-boats and only 38 decked sailing vessels. By 1905, the number of open boats was almost halved and sailing vessels had increased more than fourfold. But by 1927, the latter were no longer used. The first motor boat came into use in 1902, the first trawler in 1904.

2. Whale-catchers are excluded. In 1965 and 1967, there were 7 such boats registered, with a total gross registered tonnage of 2,858. But not all of them were in operation.

3. Also excluded are vessels under 12 gross registered tonnage. In 1963, for example, there numbered in this tonnage-group 188 decked vessels and 14–1500 open motor vessels, many of which were pleasure-craft.

4. Exact comparisons and trends in the fishing fleet had previously been hard to identify due to differences of coverage, while published sources can differ markedly. I am very grateful, therefore, to Mar Elisson, Director of Fisheries, for this table, which he has kindly updated from the analysis in *Iceland Review*, 1964. It presents a clear picture of the contemporary situation and the way it has evolved.

Source: *Maritime Register*, updated by Mar Elisson.

TABLE 2

Gross added value of Iceland's fish-processing
(including packaging and other materials)

Fish Type	1960 percentage	1965 percentage
Frozen whitefish	90	115
Frozen herring	180	230
Dry fish	50	70
Dry saltfish	158	} 125
Wet saltfish	90	
Salted herring	382	393

Source: Economic Institute, Reykjavík.

TABLE 3

Distribution of herring-catch off Icelandic coasts, 1946–64
(percentage of total catch)

	1946	*1950*	*1955*	*1960*	*1964*
North Iceland	93·8	29·2	59·9	46·6	21·7
East Iceland	0·0	0·5	5·5	15·3	61·8
South-west Iceland	6·2	70·3	34·6	38·1	16·5

Source: Iceland Herring Board.

TABLE 4

Icelandic whitefish export markets, 1946–65
(percentage sales)

	1946–50	*1951–55*	*1956–60*	*1961–65*
Britain	30	6	4	16
United States	15	43	30	53
Soviet Union	15	25	41	23
Others	40	26	25	8

Source: "Quick-Freezing Plants Association", *Iceland Review*, No. 1, Vol. v, 1967.

TABLE 5

Iceland's fish-catch by types of fish, 1960–67 (in tons)

	Herring	Cod	Haddock	Redfish (Ocean perch)	Saithe	Others	Totals
1960	136,438	304,245	42,145	59,099	12,795	38,267	592,989
1961	325,911	286,670	51,358	28,532	14,808	40,629	707,908
1962	478,127	223,449	54,276	22,273	13,469	40,490	832,084
1963	395,166	249,068	51,606	35,373	14,712	45,044	781,969
1964	544,396	280,703	56,689	27,759	21,793	40,174	971,514
1965	762,933	243,748	53,589	29,911	24,902	83,949	1,199,032
1966	769,152	231,413	35,870	23,109	20,988	157,913	1,238,445
1967	461,500	204,272	37,999	29,906	29,034	133,317	896,028

As % of total catch

	Herring	Cod	Haddock	Redfish (Ocean perch)	Saithe	Others	Totals
1964	56·0	28·9	5·8	2·8	2·2	4·3	
1966	62·1	18·7	2·9	1·9	1·7	12·7	
1967	51·5	22·8	4·3	3·3	3·2	14·9	

Source: Fisheries Association of Iceland, and Economic Institute, Reykjavik.

TABLE 6

Utilisation of the Iceland's fish-catch, 1964 and 1966
(percentage of total catch)

	1964	*1966*
Fish and herring on ice	4·1	2·3
Fish for freezing	18·9	13·2
Fish for drying (stockfish)	8·7	4·3
Fish for canning	—	—
Fish for salting	9·3	6·7
Herring for freezing	2·7	2·0
Herring for salting	5·9	5·2
Herring for meal and oil	48·3	64·8
Fish for meal and oil	0·4	0·2
Domestic fish consumption	1·4	0·9
Shellfish for freezing	0·3	0·4
Shellfish for canning	—	—

Source: Fisheries Association of Iceland, and Economic Institute, Reykjavík.

TABLE 7

Fish-catch by all nations in Icelandic waters, 1954–66
(metric tons wet weight)

Total Yield	1954	1955	1956	1957	1958†	1961†	1966†
All demersal fish	881,147	820,008	767,013	743,316	938,000	1,142,000	1,257,000
Cod	546,252	536,768	482,164	453,036	—	—	—
Haddock*	62,056	64,341	61,898	76,413	—	—	—
Plaice*	5,663	7,733	7,888	9,603	—	—	—
Redfish	141,124	110,269	92,899	84,122	—	—	—

* Close-in-shore fish, already protected.

† Figures for these years include the herring catch, which in 1956 was roughly one-eighth of the total catch, but has since accounted for all the increase in the total catch. The 1968 estimates suggest that this trend may have been slightly reversed.

Source: For 1954–57, British Aggression in Icelandic Waters, Reykjavik 1959; for 1958, 1961, 1966 Economic Institute, Reykjavik.

TABLE 8

Cod-catch: all Nations, and English, 1920–57

	Total catch all countries (000 metric tons)	English vessels catch per unit effort (cwt. per 100 ton-hours)
Av. 1920–24	217	2·41
Av. 1925–29	315	2·03
Av. 1930–34	485	2·38
Av. 1935–38	324	2·16
1950	321	1·96
1951	327	1·89
1952	392	1·83
1953	515	2·22
1954	546	2·03
1955	537	2·09
1956	482	2·05
1957	n.a.	1·89

The cod-catch is approximately 64 per cent of the total demersal catch.

Source: International Council for the Exploration of the Sea.

TABLE 9

British white-fish catch in Icelandic waters, 1951–58
(to nearest 100 cwts.)

1951	2,829,000
1952	2,489,000
1953	4,036,000
1954	3,923,000
1955	3,324,000
1956	3,027,000
1957	3,465,000
1958	3,642,000

Source: Ministry of Agriculture, Fisheries and Food, London.

TABLE 10

Belgian, English and Scottish steam-trawler catches, 1956, 1957
(average yield per 100 trawling hours, in kilos)

	Belgian		English		Scottish	
	1956	*1957*	*1956*	*1977*	*1956*	*1957*
Total	70,063	61,936	89,635	76,389	59,858	39,023
ratio 56/57	*100*	*88*	*100*	*85*	*100*	*65*
Cod	22,604	19,553	64,776	53,834	37,843	29,770
ratio 56/57	*100*	*87*	*100*	*83*	*100*	*79*
Haddock	16,473	13,209	11,832	10,687	12,165	19,425
ratio 56/57	*100*	*80*	*100*	*90*	*100*	*160*
Plaice	651	291	3,469	2,830	242	349
ratio 56/57	*100*	*45*	*100*	*82*	*100*	*144*

Source: British Aggression in Icelandic Waters, Reykjavík 1959.

TABLE 11

Landings of fish in Britain by British vessels, 1958–67

	'000 cwt	*£ '000*
1958	17,820	52,062
1959	17,700	52,460
1960	16,602	53,056
1961	15,500	51,634
1962	16,309	51,323
1963	16,771	53,583
1964	16,900	57,231
1965	18,232	60,959
1966	18,700	61,766
1967	17,801	60,972

Source: Ministry of Agriculture, Fisheries and Food, London.

TABLE 12

Iceland's exports by major commodity groups (f.o.b.), 1962–66
(in million dollars, with percentage of total)

	1962 $	1962 %	1963 $	1963 %	1964 $	1964 %	1965 $	1965 %	1966 $	1966 %
Fish and fish products										
Frozen (white)	21·4	25·4	21·8	23·2	26·8	24·1	29·0	22·4	28·1	19·9
Herring meal	7·3	8·6	10·2	10·8	13·8	12·4	22·0	17·0	26·0	18·5
Salted herring	10·9	12·9	12·8	13·6	12·0	10·8	11·4	8·8	13·6	9·7
Dried and uncured salted	9·0	10·7	7·2	7·7	9·8	8·8	10·2	7·9	12·7	9·0
Herring oil	5·6	6·6	7·0	7·4	9·7	8·7	15·8	12·8	20·5	14·6
Stockfish	6·6	7·8	6·5	6·9	7·9	7·1	8·8	6·8	7·2	5·1
Iced fish	4·0	4·7	4·7	5·0	5·1	4·6	4·6	3·6	3·7	2·6
Fish meal	3·0	3·6	2·8	3·0	3·9	3·5	3·1	2·4	3·0	2·1
Frozen herring	3·3	3·1	4·9	5·2	3·0	2·7	3·8	2·9	4·0	2·8
Cod liver oil	0·9	1·1	1·5	1·6	2·0	1·8	1·5	1·2	1·1	0·8
Whale oil	0·3	0·4	0·6	0·6	0·9	0·8	0·7	0·5	0·5	0·4
Canned fish	0·5	0·6	0·4	0·4	0·5	0·4	0·8	0·6	1·1	0·8
Redfish meal	0·1	0·1	0·4	0·4	0·3	0·3	0·6	0·5	0·4	0·4
Miscellaneous	4·6	5·4	5·8	6·2	6·8	6·1	10·1	7·8	8·3	5·9
Total fish	77·3	91·6	86·6	92·0	102·5	92·1	122·4	94·6	130·2	92·5
Agricultural products										
Hides, skins, furs	2·6	3·1	2·7	2·9	3·2	2·9	2·4	1·9	3·1	2·2
Dairy produce	0·2	0·2	0·4	0·4	1·2	1·1	0·9	0·7	1·0	0·7
Frozen mutton, lamb	1·3	1·6	1·2	1·3	1·1	1·0	0·8	0·6	1·1	0·8
Wool	1·1	1·3	0·6	0·6	0·4	0·4	0·4	0·3	0·3	0·2
Salted mutton, lamb	0·2	0·2	0·3	0·3	0·3	0·3	0·4	0·3	0·1	0·1
Miscellaneous	0·5	0·6	0·7	0·8	0·5	0·4	1·1	0·8	1·7	1·2
Total agricultural	5·9	7·0	5·9	6·3	6·7	6·1	6·0	4·6	7·3	5·2
Other Commodities	1·2	1·4	1·6	1·7	2·0	1·8	1·1	0·8	3·2	2·3
Total exports	84·4	100·0	94·1	100·0	111·2	100·0	129·5	100·0	140·7	100·0

Source: First Boston Corporation, 1966; and Economic Institute, Reykjavík, 1968.

TABLE 13

Iceland's imports by major commodity groups (c.i.f.), 1962–67
(in million dollars, with percentage of total)

	1962 $	%	1963 $	%	1964 $	%	1965 $	%	1966 $	%	1967 $	%
Fuels, lubricants etc.	11·4	12·7	12·4	11·3	12·3	9·4	12·4	9·0	12·3	7·7	13·1	8·7
Food	8·3	9·3	9·2	8·4	12·0	9·2	12·4	9·0	12·5	7·9	12·7	7·8
Machinery (non-electric)	7·9	8·9	11·9	10·9	11·5	8·8	12·2	9·6	18·1	11·4	17·8	11·0
Ships	3·9	4·4	8·6	7·9	11·4	8·7	7·3	5·3	5·9	3·7	10·7	6·6
Aircraft	0·7	0·8	0·2	0·2	10·7	8·2	6·2	4·5	6·8	4·3	5·4	3·3
Electric machinery, etc.	4·9	5·5	6·4	5·8	8·3	6·3	8·7	6·3	12·0	7·5	12·2	7·5
Transportation equipment (excl. ships and aircraft)	6·5	7·3	9·3	8·5	7·3	5·6	9·0	6·6	13·5	8·5	11·8	7·3
Wood, lumber, cork	6·2	7·0	7·2	6·6	6·7	5·1	6·7	4·9	8·6	5·4	8·2	5·0
Fishing nets and gear	3·5	3·9	4·3	3·9	5·0	3·8	5·8	4·2	6·7	4·2	5·0	3·1
Clothing, footwear	2·8	3·1	3·7	3·4	4·9	3·7	5·6	4·1	6·9	4·3	6·5	4·0
Textile yarn, fabric, etc.	5·4	6·1	4·3	3·9	4·8	3·7	5·6	4·1	5·5	3·5	5·1	3·1
Iron, steel	4·4	4·9	4·1	3·7	4·1	3·1	5·0	3·6	5·0	3·1	5·5	3·4
Paper, paperboard, etc.	2·5	2·8	3·5	3·2	4·0	3·1	4·5	3·3	4·7	2·9	4·7	2·7
Metal products	3·3	3·7	3·5	3·2	3·8	2·9	5·1	3·7	5·9	3·7	7·2	4·4
Explosives, chemicals	1·3	1·5	2·0	1·8	2·6	2·0	3·1	2·3	3·7	2·3	3·7	2·3
Tobacco, beverages	1·9	2·1	2·2	2·0	2·2	1·7	2·7	2·0	3·2	2·0	3·3	2·0
Fertilisers	1·4	1·6	1·6	1·5	1·8	1·4	2·1	1·5	1·8	1·1	2·0	1·2
Crude rubber, r. products	1·6	1·8	1·6	1·5	1·7	1·3	2·5	1·8	2·5	1·6	2·4	1·5
Animal feed stuffs	1·0	1·1	0·9	0·8	1·2	0·9	1·4	1·0	1·3	0·8	3·1	1·9
Other imports	10·3	11·5	12·8	11·5	14·7	11·1	18·0	13·2	22·4	14·1	22·1	13·6
Total imports	89·2	100·0	109·7	100·0	131·0	100·0	137·3	100·0	159·3	100·0	162·5	100·0

Source: First Boston Corporation, 1966; and Economic Institute, Reykjavík 1968.

TABLE 14

Iceland's balance of payments, 1960–67
(in million dollars)

	1960	1961	1962	1963	1964	1965	1966	1967
Balance on current a/c	0·0	0·0	0·0	−4·3	−7·9	−5·1	−8·2	−44·2
Over-all balance	0·0	0·0	0·0	3·8	6·5	7·4	0·0	−26·6
Convertible currencies	0·0	0·0	0·0	2·7	10·1	11·6	1·4	0·0
Clearing currencies	0·0	0·0	0·0	1·1	−3·6	−4·2	−1·4	0·0
Total net foreign-exchange reserves, gov't and private	3·0	12·3	26·8	30·5	37·1	42·0	0·0	0·0

Source: OECD *Economic Survey*, January 1968; and Central Bank of Iceland.

TABLE 15

Gross National product and income, 1962–68
(1960 prices)

	1962	1963	1964	1965	1966	1967	1968 (est.)
	(Annual Growth Rates)						
Gross national product	8·0	7·1	5·4	5·0	3·5	−1·5	−2·8
Effects of changes in terms of trade	0·7	0·4	3·2	4·9	0·6	−7·4	−2·1
Gross national income	8·4	7·2	8·3	9·2	3·7	−8·0	−4·7

Source: OECD *Economic Survey*, January 1969; and Central Bank of Iceland.

TABLE 16

Gross fixed asset formation, 1962–68
(constant 1960 prices)

	1962	1963	1964	1965	1966	1967 (prov.)	1968 (est.)
As percentage change from previous year	16·9	30·7	17·6	−0·6	14·9	11·8	−6·5

Source: OECD *Economic Survey*, January 1969; and Economic Institute Reykjavík.

TABLE 17

Ordinary revenues of central government, 1960–67 (million kronur)

	1960	1961	1962	1963	1964	1965	1966	1967 (budget)
Indirect Taxes								
General ad. val. import duties	733·4	850·9	1,108·5	1,331·9	1,414·9	1,608·3	1,937·7	1,445·7
Specific duties on petrol	57·1	55·2	58·4	62·4	*	—	189·0	173·2
Special car import duty	15·0	40·7	65·2	123·3	119·5	125·3	—	—
Motor vehicle tax	16·7	18·2	21·8	25·6	0·9*	—	—	—
Domestic sales tax	142·4	168·1	193·4	234·3	544·2	937·8	1,138·5	1,221·9
Excise taxes	35·0	36·7	42·1	48·2	52·3	54·8	60·8	60·0
Stamp tax	38·0	40·5	47·7	57·7	69·0	80·6	90·1	95·0
Bank transactions tax	14·0	18·8	23·5	20·3	31·2	21·8	68·8	66·5
Insurance premiums tax	10·7	1·5	0·5	0·1	0·3	—	—	—
Total Indirect Taxes	1,062·4	1,230·9	1,561·1	1,903·8	2,232·3	2,826·6	3,484·9	3,445·7
Profits from state monopolies and enterprises	271·2	271·3	306·1	360·8	379·1	425·2	618·2	558·4
Direct Taxes								
Income and property tax	96·8	106·1	118·8	182·5	259·2	365·8	470·6	603·0
Surtax on profits	2·3	—	—	—	—	—	—	—
Total Direct Taxes	96·8	106·1	118·8	182·5	259·2	365·8	470·6	603·0
Miscellaneous Revenues	49·4	51·3	56·7	56·2	61·9	64·6	82·1	90·2
Interest	5·6	5·0	8·8	14·1	13·9	8·3	22·0	8·0
Total Ordinary Revenues	1,487·7	1,664·6	2,051·5	2,517·4	2,946·4	3,690·5	4,677·8	4,705·3

* In 1964, a Road Fund was established into which all petrol and motor vehicle taxes are paid and which provides for all expenditure on road construction and maintenance.

Source: First Boston Corporation, 1966; and Economic Institute, Reykjavik 1968.

TABLE 18

Ordinary expenditure of central government, 1960–67
(million kronur)

	1960	1961	1962	1963	1964	1965	1966	1967 (budget)
General Administration	161·7	172·4	207·1	257·7	322·8	390·5	471·0	503·3
Economic and Social Services								
Public health	41·7	51·5	69·3	86·2	100·8	133·5	171·4	216·2
Transport, communications	160·6	174·3	201·2	246·0	191·7	189·2	163·3	178·1
Church, education, science	199·1	216·1	266·2	366·6	479·8	588·7	675·0	801·8
Agriculture	76·2	74·7	81·7	101·8	132·8	213·3	214·9	225·5
Fisheries and industry	29·4	31·0	34·4	68·3	67·7	163·1	175·1	258·2
Electric power	36·5	32·3	32·8	31·6	50·0	76·8	49·8	53·1
Social security	319·8	377·7	421·9	511·8	705·5	776·5	897·2	1,106·9
Pensions	28·9	32·8	41·2	51·2	63·4	76·9	95·9	102·3
Consumer subsidies	259·8	305·8	346·3	342·2	363·9	511·4	613·1	708·0
Agricultural export subsidies	5·0	21·1	31·8	87·0	217·3	167·8	248·0	248·0
Miscellaneous	11·5	14·5	19·2	22·7	217·7	116·4	116·2	51·0
Investment expenditures on "capital account"	68·6	61·9	63·1	75·1	111·5	124·4	130·6	179·7
Interest Paid	2·1	6·4	2·8	4·4	6·0	9·1	8·3	11·0
Total Ordinary Expenditures	1,400·9	1,571·7	1,819·0	2,252·7	3,030·9	3,537·9	4,029·8	4,634·1

Source: First Boston Corporation, 1966; and Economic Institute, Reykjavík 1968

TABLE 19

Yearly average earnings, 1960–66
(1960 = 100)

	1960	1961	1962	1963	1964	1965	1966
Unskilled workers	100·0	105·3	126·3	154·7	202·9	246·8	298·0
Skilled workers	100·0	105·9	130·4	158·4	202·2	250·2	300·0
Seamen	100·0	120·3	143·6	163·4	219·3	279·2	304·2
All workers and seamen	100·0	108·2	131·2	158·2	204·8	252·7	300·7

Source: OECD *Economic Survey,* January 1968.

TABLE 20

Variations in the value of the Icelandic krona, 1946–68

Effective from	Parity with Us $
December 18, 1946	6·48885
September 21, 1949	9·34107
March 20, 1950	16·2857
February 22, 1960	38·0
August 4, 1961	43·0
November 24, 1967	57·0
November 1, 1968	88·0

Source: First Boston Corporation, 1966; and Economic Institute, Reykjavik.

References

1. The Beautiful Nightmare

1. Sigurdur Thorarinsson, *Fire and Ice*, Reykjavík 1959.
2. Jörgen Mindelberg, cited in Sigurdur Thorarinsson, *Surtsey*, Reykjavík 1964.
3. Anon., *An Historical and Descriptive Account of Iceland, Greenland and the Pharoes*, Edinburgh 1840, p. 19.
4. Cf. Thorarinsson, *Fire and Ice*, op. cit.
5. *An Historical and Descriptive Account . . .*, op. cit., p. 30 ff.

2. Commonwealth and Colony

1. Those interested in further study of this point should refer to Sir William Craigie's article, "The Gaels in Iceland", in *Proceedings of the Society of Antiquaries in Scotland*, Edinburgh 1896–97, p. 247; also his "Gaelic Words and Names in Icelandic Sagas", in *Zeitschrift für Keltische Philologie*, Vol. I, p. 439 *ff.*
2. *The Libelle of Englyshe Polycye*, Sir George Warren (ed.), Oxford University Press, London 1926, l. 792 et seq.
3. For a full account of the co-operative movement, see Thorsten Odhe, *Iceland: The Co-operative Island*, Co-operative League of the USA, Chicago 1960.
4. Odhe, op. cit., p. 49.
5. Ibid., p. 51.
6. Ibid., p. 52.

215

Modern Iceland

3. If the Fish Should Swim Away . . .

1. For much of the information on the fish-freezing industry in this chapter, I am indebted to Gudmundur Gardarsson.
2. In a letter to the author.

4. The Search for Economic Security

1. J. E. Cross, *A Yacht Voyage to Iceland*, London 1858, p. 12.
2. Charles Babbage, *The Economy of Machinery and Manufacture*, 2nd edn, London 1832, p. 384.
3. Jonas Haralz and Arni Vilhjalmsson, *The Economic Development of Iceland*, Reykjavík 1960.

6. The 'Cod War' and International Relations

1. *The Times*, September 26, 1951.
2. Ibid., October 6, 1951.
3. Ibid., December 15, 1951.
4. Cf. the Central Office of Information's booklet No. R4872, HMSO, London 1961.

7. The Last Civilisation

1. In conversation with the author.
2. Ibid.
3. Ibid.
4. Guthmunder Finbogasson, *Iceland 1946*, National Bank of Iceland, Reykjavík 1946.
5. For an excellent discussion of humour in the Sagas, see R. W. Wilson, "Comedy of Character in the Icelandic Family Sagas", in D. A. Pearsall and R. A. Waldron (eds.), *Medieval Literature and Civilization: Studies in Memory of G. N. Garmonsway*, Athlone Press, London 1969. The quotation on page 162 of our text occurs in the context of Mr Wilson's discussion of *Grettis Saga*.
6. *An Historical and Descriptive Account* . . ., op. cit., p. 88.
7. In conversation with the author.
8. Sigurdur Nordal, *Bibliography of Old Norse–Icelandic Studies*, Munksgaard, Copenhagen 1960, p. 10.
9. In conversation with the author.
10. Nordal, op. cit., p. 13.

Short Reading List

A scholarly and detailed history of Iceland until the nineteenth century is given by the anonymous author of *An Historical Description of Iceland, Greenland and the Pharoes*, Edinburgh 1840. The best brief modern account is to be found in Laxness, Thorarinsson and Nawrath, *Iceland: A Heroic Landscape*, Kummel Frey, Berne 1962. This also contains some beautiful full-plate illustrations of Iceland's striking landscape. A good comprehensive account of Iceland is the supposedly secret publication written for British officers in the last war.

A short, if rather technical, survey of Iceland's geology is Sigurdur Thorarinsson (ed.), *On the Geology and Geophysics of Iceland*, International Geological Congress, Reykjavík 1960. The same author's *Surtsey*, Almenna Bokafelageth, Reykjavík 1964, is a succinct and well-illustrated account of Iceland's most recent marine eruption, which created the new island from which the book takes its title. For a general geography, the reader is referred to Axel Sømme (ed.), *A Geography of Norden*, Heinemann, London 1960.

For translations of the Sagas, Heimskringla and other Icelandic literature, Dent's 'Everyman Library' caters well. Gwyn Jones has translated *Egils Saga*, Syracuse University Press, Syracuse N.Y. 1960; and *The Saga of Erik the Red*, Oxford University Press, London and New York 1961. For a modern translation of *Njáls Saga*, that by M. Magnusson and H. Palsson, Penguin, Harmondsworth and Baltimore 1960, is recommended. For general background to Icelandic literature, see: H. R. Ellis Davidson, *Gods and Myths of Northern Europe*, Penguin, Harmondsworth and Baltimore 1964; and G. Turville-Petre, *Origins of Icelandic Literature*, Oxford University Press,

Modern Iceland

London and New York 1953. A more rhapsodic view can be found in Samivel's, *L'Or de l'Iseland*, Arthaud, Paris 1963.

For general background information until 1946, particularly economic, consult *Iceland 1946*, published by the National Bank of Iceland. A new edition is overdue and should prove equally valuable when published. In regard to more up-to-date economic information, all the salient points and statistical tables are given in the annual surveys published both by the Icelandic Economic Institute in Reykjavík and also by the OECD in Paris. A useful brief economic summary is to be found in a paper written for the Economic Institute: Jonas Haralz and Arni Vilhjamsson, *The Economic Development of Iceland*, 1960.

The *Icelandic Review*, available quarterly on subscription, gives a regular picture of events of all kinds in contemporary Iceland.

Among the great literary travellers to Iceland may be noted: Richard Burton, *Ultima Thule*, London and Edinburgh 1875; William Morris, *Journal of Travels in Iceland*, Collected Works, Vol. VIII, London 1911; W. H. Auden and Louis McNiece, *Letters from Iceland*, London 1937.

For modern Icelandic literature, translations of seven of Halldor Laxness's novels are available, and as is on two of Thor Vilhjalmsson's.

Halldor Laxness's are: *Salka Valka*, Allen and Unwin, London 1936; Houghton Mifflin, Boston 1936. *Independent People*, Allen and Unwin, London 1945; Alfred Knopf, New York 1946. *The Happy Warriors*, Methuen, London 1958. *The Honour of the House*, Helgafell, Reykjavík 1959. *The Atom Station*, Methuen, London 1961. *Paradise Reclaimed*, Methuen, London 1962; Thomas Crowell, New York 1962. *The Fish Can Sing*, Methuen, London 1966; Thomas Crowell, New York 1967.

Thor Vilhjalmsson's are: *Faces Reflected in a Drop*, Helgafell, Reykjavík 1966. *Quick Quick Said the Bird*, and *Kjarval* are in process of translation.

Index

Act of Union (1918), 40–1
Africa, stockfish exports to, 51–2
Agrarian party, 103
Agriculture, *see* Farming
Airlines and airfields, 72, 77–8,
   84–5; Iceland as transatlantic
   staging post, 167
Akureyrí, 47, 76–7, 99
Algerian pirates, 45
Althing (parliament), 27–35, 81,
   102, 147, 181*ff.*; abolished (1801)
   then re-established (1843–5),38–
   40; composition of, 108–9, 186–8;
   judiciary, 192–3; powers and
   procedure, 108–9, 188–92; two
   chambers of, 108, 187–8; sessions
   in verse, 174
Althythublathith, 121
Aluminium-smelting project, 81–3
Arason, Jon, bishop of Holar, 27, 37
Arnarson, Ingólfur, 20–2
Arts, visual, 162, 169–74, 179–80
Asa faith, 23, 33–4
Ashe, Geoffrey, 19n.
Askja volcano, 7–9
Astronauts, training ground for, 7

Athens, Iceland compared with, 32
Atom Station, The, 152

Babbage, Charles, 80–1
Bananas, culture of, 70, 173
Barthastrand, 74
Belgium, protests against fishing
   limits, 136
Benediksson, Bjarni, 64, 96, 144
Bjarnasson, Sigurdur, 110, 112–13
Black Death, 16
Blakeney (Norfolk), 43
Blood feuds, 23
Bodvarsson, Gudmundur, 166
Brandur (trawler), 144
Brendan, Saint, 10–11, 18–19
Bristol, 43
Britain: dispute with Iceland ('cod
   war'), 135–45; fishing industry,
   130–1 (*see also* Cod war *and* App.
   II, tables 8–11); Icelanders' atti-
   tude to, 151; occupation of Ice-
   land (1940), 40–2, 85, 87, 112;
   quarrel with Norway re fishing
   zones, 133; trade and piracy in

219